Heroes, Rogues,
and the Rest

LIVES THAT
– TELL –
THE STORY OF
THE BIBLE

Heroes, Rogues, and the Rest

J. ELLSWORTH KALAS

Abingdon Press / *Nashville*

HEROES, ROGUES, AND THE REST
LIVES THAT TELL THE STORY OF THE BIBLE

Copyright © 2014 by Abingdon Press

All rights reserved.

Library of Congress Cataloging-in-Publication Data

Kalas, J. Ellsworth, 1923-
    Heroes, rogues, and the rest : lives that tell the story of the Bible / J. Ellsworth Kalas.
        pages cm.
    Includes bibliographical references.
    ISBN 978-1-4267-7562-8 (binding: soft back; adhesive perfect binding : alk. paper)   1. Bible—Biography.   I.   Title.
    BS571.K28 2014
    220.9′2—dc23
    [B]

                                                    2013034828

14 15 16 17 18 19 20 21 22 23—10 9 8 7 6 5 4 3 2 1
MANUFACTURED IN THE UNITED STATES OF AMERICA

Contents

Contents

Introduction

A great many years ago I found a seat in Bascom Hall of the University of Wisconsin to begin a yearlong course in American history. Like most students of my generation I had studied the history of my nation intermittently since I was in the fourth grade. The study had been a mixed bag, sometimes tedious, sometimes exciting, but generally short on plot.

This course was different. William Best Hesseltine told us the history of America via personalities. All kinds of personalities: heroes and rogues and the mix that leaves it to historians to decide which. There were soldiers and poets and preachers; scholars and rabble-rousers; fortune-builders and reformers; idealists and scam artists. But leave out any of these people and America would not be America. Perhaps the basic plot would still be there, but if the plot were conveyed via an opera there would be a serious dissonance in the music unless all these characters played their parts.

I don't remember if Professor Hesseltine told us that Thomas Carlyle wrote, "History is the essence of innumerable biographies," or that almost a generation later Ralph Waldo Emerson said, "There is properly no history; only biography," or that Benjamin Disraeli—who made a bit of history himself—insisted, "Read no history; nothing but biography, for that is life without theory." But quote them or not, the venerable Wisconsin historian demonstrated their truth. When the year of classes ended, I understood American history with a depth, breadth, and vitality I had never gotten before.

It's on the basis of that classroom experience and a lifetime of reading, loving, preaching, and teaching the Bible that I now attempt to put the Bible's story into a series of biographies. I dare to hope that this is a special, helpful way to convey the eternal story, even though I know it is limited by my own inadequacies.

Certainly the Bible is the most fascinating collection of biographies to be found anywhere. They may seem to come helter-skelter, they may startle us with their utter transparency, and they may drive us to both wonder and despair. But if we pay attention to them, we will be changed because these stories not only inform, if given half a chance they also transform. And they've been doing so for centuries, at every level of culture, every age, and at qualities of perception both grand and mundane.

Let me underline what is probably obvious, that the Bible is the most honest of books. It never tries to protect its characters, never leaves "the warts and all" out of their portraits. What they were is what you see and get. If they make you draw in your breath in shock, so be it. And if they make you feel that they've given you a taste of God's hope for our human race, take that, too. But know that you're never being lied to.

So join me now as we watch the Heroes, the Rogues, and the Rest, and see for yourself.

CHAPTER 1

In the Beginning, God

The Bible story begins with God. Singularly so. There are no other characters until God creates them, so if we're to tell the Bible story via biography, we have to begin with God.

Of course it's audacious to become a biographer of God, but it's not without precedent. There have always been persons—some of them professional scholars and some street-corner philosophers—who contend that our human perception of God is a product of our own imaginative concocting. I don't subscribe to that point of view, but I recognize that to a degree all of us who think about God (which is all of us, at one time or another) craft our own versions, made up partly of inherited views and then both refined and clouded by our own experiences and prejudices.

But I don't plan to start a biography of God from scratch, and although I hope to tell the story in ways that will make it more accessible and more intimately real, I intend to get my data from the Scriptures of the Old and New Testaments; after all, I'm promising to give you a study of the Bible via biographies so I'm obligated to stay within the Bible. The Bible is a directory of names—hundreds upon hundreds of them, with an astonishing variety. But in a sense, there are only two characters in all of the Bible's wonderful, sprawling plot: God and all those other names.

So my series of biographies must begin with God because God is the one continuing character. Even in the book of Esther, where God is never specifically mentioned, every reader knows that God is the brooding eminence who will somehow make sense of all that unfolds. Even in some of the psalms and in parts of Job and Ecclesiastes, when God seems primarily an object of complaint, still God is the continuing fact and future.

This God of the Scriptures is a God who acts—not necessarily when the parties of the second part want the action and quite often not in the kind of action that ensues. No matter, the action is there. When some biblical writers report God's activity they sound like nature poets, whereas others seem like graduates of a military academy. Some are sentimental almost to a fault, and others are so matter-of-fact that they seem without heart. Whatever the case, the biblical writers report primarily on God's activity. They use occasional adjectives to describe God—such as righteous, holy, just, and kind—but their portrayal comes primarily from God's activity. That's why their picture of God is so fascinating yet also so unnerving.

In the process of reporting God's activity, the biblical biographers also give us a variety of names for God, names coming from particular human experiences. Thus, a slave girl in life-and-death trouble knows God as El Roi (God who sees, or God whom I've seen, Genesis 16:13), and for a patriarch about to give up, God becomes El Shaddai (God Almighty, Genesis 17:1). Later this patriarch, now even older, experiences God as El Olam (the eternal God, Genesis 21:33). Figures of speech enrich the biography still more, as God is to some a fortress, to others a father or a mother, and still to others a close kin who can redeem from trouble.

What the Bible biographers don't tell us is where God came from. This is one of the key evidences of their sublime wisdom. It's the beginning, and God is *here*, and that's it. It's as if the biblical writers think it's beneath God to tell of God's origins. Or perhaps they're only confessing that they don't know and they don't intend to tell us what they don't know. In any event, unlike many of us, they don't think it's an important question. They know that there is a God, and they consider someone a fool who thinks otherwise (Psalm 14:1). If God be God, there can be nothing before; if there were something preceding God that something would be God, and anything that followed would be derivative. God is the Grand Original; that is, the utter Origin. All else finds its origin in God; some of it, it seems, in a spiral of descent that is quite unlike its origin.

God is powerful. This is clear before the biblical biography is into the second paragraph. At this early point in the story, whatever God wants God gets. A little later God's special creation, humanity (all those "other names"), having been given a mind of its own, begins to complicate the scene. This is when the plot becomes really exciting yet also really frustrating. But at the outset, God has only to speak for things to happen: light, separation of waters, plant life, animal life, humanity—and God is pleased with it all. I like that. I would hate for God to be systemically dissatisfied. I like the fact that the Bible's biography of God shows God at pleasure and that one of Jesus's parables describing the consummation of all things pictures God saying to the best of us, "Well done." This is wonderfully encouraging, something to fall asleep on each night, that God has a capacity for satisfaction, even in dealing with us errant humans.

I like the *way* God creates, speaking everything into existence. I like this because of what it tells us about the kind of God we're doing business with. We have a communicating God, one who honors the creation by speaking to it with words. I have great respect for geniuses in engineering, mathematics, and construction, and unskilled as I am, I often envy them. But I like having a God whose primary means of action and relationship is communication. Words. By extension this tells me I should be more careful about the words I use and the way I use them. Because if God got everything going by way of words, I recognize that we humans can get everything messed up by the way we use words.

It's also clear that God knows who is in charge. Kilian McDonnell, the Benedictine scholar-poet, pictures Abraham accusing God of being "imperious." The answer is, "Why not?" God is the only one with the right to be imperious, and at particular times of trouble, we humans come stumbling to God with our appeal to exercise some of that imperial power. As the one in charge, God tells us humans early in the story where the boundaries are. And we humans, being human, set out shortly to test not simply the boundaries but the authority of the one who declares the boundaries as well.

It's at this point that we discover what we need most in God; that God is gracious. When the humans (man and woman—it takes both of us to mess things up) test God's authority, God does not allow us to go on our erratic ways unhampered; with infinite humility, God pursues the humans. With their sin, the humans go into hiding, covering themselves with fig leaves, a quite insubstantial effort since the leaves will so quickly wither. They also hide themselves "among the trees of the garden." But God pursues them.

Of course this is very easy for God to do. God has an advantage on us in the nature of our makeup, by breathing divine breath in us and by making us in the divine image. Thus we can't escape from God because the breath is there—and the only way to escape our breath is to die. And then what? The biblical poet (one of us humans) got it right when he wept,

> Where can I go from your spirit?
> Or where can I flee from your presence?
> If I ascend to heaven, you are there;
> if I make my bed in Sheol [death]
> you are there.
> (Psalm 139:7-8 NRSV)

Nineteenth-century poet Francis Thompson said that he had fled God "down the labyrinthine ways / Of my own mind"— and of course that's the point: when we flee God through our own minds we find that we've simply moved into occupied territory.[1] God was here first, in the quality and reality of our breath.

(You may have noticed that I have slipped momentarily from the biography of God to the biography of the rest of us, the humans. I'll be guilty of this lapse repeatedly because while our first chapter is a biography of God, God will reappear in every chapter that follows, even when those chapters seem primarily about human beings. By the same token, I can't say much about God without bringing us humans into the story. This is partly because we know God best through his dealings with us even though the Bible makes clear that God has a great deal to do besides carry on business with us humans. Furthermore, the Bible gives the impression that in spite of all God has to do with this continuously expanding universe, God cares most about what happens to us humans. That's a major theme in the plot of the biblical story. In this regard, the Bible is a very heady, exciting, and exalting book for humans to read because it indicates that humans are so uniquely important.)

When I interrupted myself I was saying that God is gracious, as demonstrated in God's pursuing us. See the way God does so. He invites us to identify ourselves. "Where are you?" Here is the question we keep asking ourselves because it is God's first question to us. So our poets, playwrights, and storytellers keep asking the question, and we in turn ask our parents and counselors and psychiatrists. Then, in turn, our advertisers, inventors, and political leaders keep pressing us with their answers, even though we haven't necessarily directed the question to them. But it was God who first asked us to locate ourselves so that we would understand where we are. Because if we're going to carry on a conversation with God we need to know our own location, our own emotional, psychic, and spiritual setting.

As you can see, the gracious quality in God appears very early in the biblical biography of God. Our preaching sometimes seems to suggest that God discovered grace at Calvary. Not so. God began pursuing us human creatures as soon as we began wandering because this is the nature of God. God chooses to work with us humans, whatever our state—even when it's a state of rebellion or indifference.

The quality of God's grace is put to the test early in the story. After some fits and starts, as we shall see in the next chapter, the relationship between God and the human race comes to a particular crisis when the nastiness in humans becomes so great that "every inclination of the thoughts of their hearts was only evil continually" (Genesis 6:5). At this point God seems to wrestle with the possibility that perhaps the whole human project was a mistake. "The LORD regretted making human beings on the earth, and he was heartbroken" (Genesis 6:6).

This is one of the most fascinating sentences in the Bible, one of the most intriguing insights into the personality, nature, and character of God. The biographer in Genesis pictures God in a reflective mood so deep that God seems uncertain about his own plans. It seems to me that the Bible wants us to understand the intensity of God's pain and the majesty of his love for us humans and his expectations for our potential. If we were less, perhaps God wouldn't suffer so poignantly in our failures. I have said that God's breath in us complicates our journey because we can't escape from God; we can't escape our own breath. In turn, God's breath in us presents a problem to God, the problem of divine high expectations: this creature with God's breath ought not to stoop to base, pointless, and stupid living.

But God has a game plan. And because the plan allows for human responses, the plan sometimes seems—at least from our perspective—to change signals at the line of scrimmage. When things get so bad that God is heartbroken, God begins again with Noah. And when feisty humans start a tower at Babel, God disperses them into their original assignment to "fill the earth." Then, especially, when the whole human enterprise seems to be going nowhere in particular, God calls Abram and Sarai (Abraham and Sarah) to establish a plotline that goes through both Testaments all the way into Revelation and the consummation of all things.

I'm glad that God has a plan. I want to know that someone is at the helm in this space vehicle where we live out our lives and begin our eternal venture. The daily culture insists that life is just one fool thing after another. But the Bible's story of God insists that while our human story seems erratic and often pointless, God continues to be involved because God has a plan. This guarantees that there is purpose not only in the total human story but in the individual roles that each of us play—provided we are willing to accept our purpose. And the final purpose is divine.

Since God has a plan, God is patient. We appreciate God's patience when we are its recipients more than when we have to wait on others who are its beneficiaries. Moses needed the patience of God when God called him and he was reluctant to cooperate, but Moses found it difficult to be patient with the Israelites when they were spiritually dull.

So God stays with the remarkable people called Israel, the descendants of Abraham and Sarah, Isaac and Rebekah, and Jacob and his wives. God watches over them through centuries of slavery in Egypt, then through a pilgrimage of forty years in the wilderness, and then through roller-coaster political years with judges and kings and captivities and recoveries.

So it is that from Genesis 11:27 through the rest of the Hebrew Scriptures, the Old Testament is primarily the story of God's relationship with a particular people, the descendants of Jacob, grandson of Abraham: the people we know as Israel, or the Jews. Other nations and peoples come into the story, but only by way of their relationship to this special people. They are "chosen," but their chosenness is more responsibility and mission than favor. God often preserves them against remarkable odds and blesses them with victories in a variety of David-and-Goliath mismatches.

But with all of that, the Bible tells their story with devastating candor. If ever a series of historians told a nation's history with unblushing honesty it is the writers of the Old Testament. Several of the prophets picture the relationship of God and Israel as that of marriage; and much of the time a very stormy marriage! Israel seems to wander from God as much as, or even more than, it stays true; yet God continues to pursue them. They are the covenant people, no matter what their shortcomings, rebellions, or unfaithfulness.

God's plan and patience shows itself with particular eloquence and beauty in the ministry of the prophets. The prophets are the voice of God and the presence of God through good years and bad. It is significant that their words occupy hundreds of pages of our Bible. They tell us how awesome God is. Isaiah realizes that heaven is God's throne and the earth God's footstool, and that God "has measured the waters in the hollow of his hand / and marked off the heavens with a span" (Isaiah 40:12 NRSV). Hosea, on the other hand, tells us how vulnerable God is, this God who pleads, "How can I give you up, Ephraim? / How can I hand you over, O Israel?" (Hosea 11:8 NRSV). God has a plan, and the plan is immersed in love so that even though God is supremely powerful, he holds out with patience with the humility of divine patience.

And then, God *came*. The Word that operated in the creation process in Genesis "became flesh and lived among us, and we have seen his glory, the glory as of a father's only son, full of grace and truth" (John 1:14 NRSV). Now we see God as, at the same moment, most powerful, most loving, and most vulnerable. Most powerful because there is no power greater than the power that is ready to lay aside power; most loving because this power exercises itself to seek out the human race and save it; and most vulnerable because the power comes in human flesh: "emptied himself, / taking the form of a slave" and then, "obedient to the point of death— / even death on a cross" (Philippians 2:7-8 NRSV). And in all of this, God opens the divine Self to rejection.

This is the most telling detail in the biography of God. It goes without saying that no single incident or characteristic is adequate to describe God or to tell God's story as we humans know it. But if there is any single event in the biography that demonstrates what you and I need most to know about God, this is it: God empties himself of all power; takes on the form of a slave [our slave], in human likeness; then becomes obedient not only to death, but to death on a cross. God, the guiltless, becomes the symbol and essence of guilt.

This picture is at one with the opening scene in Genesis, when God speaks and whatever is spoken to responds. Now God uses the divine power in the act of restraint, in laying aside the power, all for the sake of pursuing the human creature. The New Testament rounds out the picture of God in what we call the Trinity—a term that does not appear as such in the Bible but that demonstrates itself in the person of Jesus the Christ and in the Holy Spirit. The Old Testament mentions the Spirit of God from time to time, but in the New Testament this element of God's action comes full front with the birth of the church at Pentecost.

In the Old Testament, the relationship of God with the whole body of humankind was implicit—first in the creation itself, then in the crises that led to the call of Abraham and the beginning of the covenant people, Israel. It was also implicit in Abraham's call; his seed was to bless "all the families of earth" (Genesis 12:3). Much of the time, unfortunately, Israel's role as God's witness to the other nations was muted by the antagonism between Jews and non-Jews.

With the birth of the church, the relationship of God with all of humanity becomes explicit. The message on the Day of Pentecost—the day we traditionally speak of as the birthday of the church—is in multiple tongues, symbolizing all peoples, and as the events of the early church unfold the boundaries of race, language, customs, and political systems gradually fall. As the apostle Paul puts it in a shocking challenge to a group of philosophers at Mars Hill in Athens, "God overlooks ignorance of these things in times past, but now directs everyone everywhere to change their hearts and lives" (Acts 17:30).

It is the church (the new Israel) that is to carry this word to the whole human race, with all its power structures. But even in the earliest days of the church, as revealed in the book of Acts and the several apostolic epistles, the church is not noticeably an improvement on Israel. The marks of human arrogance and ignorance and apathy all appear now in this body, and one wonders where the story of God will end. How can it possibly end in anything but defeat, in light of the people God uses to establish the Kingdom?

Well, as the Bible reports it, God's story will conclude in triumph. There is a city—an ultimate civilization—where "God's glory is its light." And the lamp from which the light comes (in a strange mixture of figures of speech) "is the Lamb" (Revelation 21:23). The symbol of God's willing helplessness, the Lamb, is also the symbol of God's final and complete victory. The inference is that all of creation will learn unceasingly of the marvel and mystery of God.

But you have a question. If this book is about heroes and rogues, it seems as if God is by definition a Hero. Ultimately, yes. But the Bible again is painfully honest. We humans judge our heroes and rogues mostly by how we think they're treating us, and repeatedly in the Bible story humans don't like the way God treats them. Even some of the greatest souls have their moments of crying "Why?" or "How can you do this to me (or my people)?" That is, sometimes as we read this biblical story we have to wait for another chapter (perhaps several more chapters!) to determine how others have seen God—and by extension, how we do.

So it's time to move on in the story. Time, that is, to see more of the other character in the drama, human beings.

CHAPTER 2

Adam and Eve: Our Kind of People

The Bible's biographies take a precipitous drop when we move from God to Adam and Eve. It could hardly be otherwise. God is God, the Bible reminds us regularly, and there is no other. By contrast, Adam and Eve are like the billions of human creatures who have populated and continue populating our planet. You can't really compare the two. What the Bible asks is not so much to compare, but to see how closely we're related. It does so with two pictures of our human origin. One is a theological statement, in Genesis 1; the other, in Genesis 2, is a beautiful short story.

The first is succinct, and as I said, it's theological—that is, it centers on God. It tells us why God made us human creatures:

that having made the heavens and the earth, including all of earth's furnishings, and then a spectacular variety of inhabit-ants—things that "swarm in the waters," others that "fly above the earth," livestock, wildlife, and "every kind of creature that crawls on the ground," and being pleased with it all—God now wanted a resident manager to "take charge of the fish of the sea, the birds of the sky, the livestock, all the earth, and all the crawling things on earth" (Genesis 1:26). That is, with such a creation, a manager was needed. And what kind of creature will this be?

> God created humanity
>   in God's own image,
>   in the divine image God created them,
>   male and female God created them.
>   (Genesis 1:27)

The most impressive and singular thing about us humans in this account is that we were made "in God's own image." Then the writer says it again, as if he wants to be sure that we're get-ting the point, since it's a very big point: "In the divine image God created them." This is who we are, and this is what dis-tinguishes us from the rest of earth's creatures: we are made in God's image. And from the beginning we are "male and female."

The second story still has God as the lead character, but the emphasis is on drama and poetry more than on theology. Mind you, the theology is still primary because God is as much in charge as in the first report. But this time we get it by way of a story. As we read it, we can almost see a play unfolding before us on a cosmic stage. In this telling, God makes not male and female but just a male. And where the earlier story tells us simply that we humans are made in God's image, without details of the process, this time we read that "the Lord God formed the human from the topsoil of the fertile land" (2:7): that is, that we humans belong to the earth on which we live. We are made of the same substance that produces vegetables and grass and trees. But there's more to us; dramatically more! Because "the Lord God...blew life's breath into his nostrils" (2:7). While we come out of the same soil as the grass and the trees, our life has another source. The breath that is in us is the very breath of God.

To get the full significance of this story we should remember that the Hebrew word for *breath* (that is, the Old Testament word) is also the word for *wind* or *spirit*. When we read that the breath in us humans is breathed into us by God, we realize that the spirit of God is in us. As the Bible reports it, this characteristic makes us humans unique. There is a divine investment in every human creature. Therefore, whenever we touch a human life we engage in holy business. Since human life is holy—God-breathed—to misuse it is unholy.

There's still more to come in this unfolding drama. The inspired Genesis-writer—who is part theologian, part poet, part historian, and part storyteller—wants to make a very important point about the kind of creatures we humans are. He leads into the issue indirectly, telling us that "The Lord God planted a garden in Eden in the east and put there the human he had formed" (2:8). The word *Eden* conveys the idea of Paradise. But Edenic life doesn't mean lolling under a tree while its fruit falls into the human's mouth. This human has a job in Eden, "to farm it and to take care of it" (2:15). "Eat your fill," God tells him, "but don't eat from the tree of the knowledge of good and evil" (2:17).

Thus we learn that we humans are choice-makers, and that we live in a moral universe. Our contemporary culture plays down the moral quality of our universe and the moral issues involved in being human. This is not new to our times. Any careful reading of human history shows that our attitude toward ourselves as moral creatures ebbs and flows. Some generations are more driven by a sense of moral responsibility than others. Also, our moral judgments are always uneven. Each generation emphasizes some moral issues above others, and various cultures within each generation have their own emphases. Broadly speaking, for instance, some persons and philosophies emphasize economic morality, others social morality, and still others sexual morality. But whatever the emphasis in any particular time or social or cultural group, one thing is inescapable: we humans—unlike anything else in our creation—are creatures that *choose*; and ultimately these choices are between good and evil, between the approved and the forbidden. Different persons and different philosophies produce their own definitions of good and evil, but the fact of *choice* remains. To put it another way, we humans are, by nature and by our very creation, *responsible* creatures. This is quite burdensome at times, but that's the price of being made in the image of God and of possessing (and being possessed by) the breath of God. The human who says, "I'll do as I please" has a poor view of himself and thus of the human race. To be properly human one says, "I will do what is right." To say anything less is to deny who we are: creatures made in the image of God and responsible for the choices we make.

But back to our story. God now gives the human a further job, indeed, a highly intellectual one—identifying and naming the rest of creation. The scientist is already at work, classifying the rest of the earth's inhabitants.

So the human has a paradisiacal residence and an occupation, as a matter of fact, a *calling*, a vocation from God. The human being is not only the resident manager of Eden, he is also the interpreter who is responsible for organizing all the other inhabitants of the Garden. If the human only needs food, beauty, perfect living conditions, and ego-enhancing work, this human has it made.

But it isn't so. Something vital is missing. The God who punctuated the creation story with observing how good it was now says that something is *not* good: "It's not good that the human is alone" (2:18). So the human surveys the rest of creation, but something "perfect for him was nowhere to be found" (2:20).

Everything that once seemed perfect is suddenly inadequate. But don't fret. The solution is close at hand and quite logical: take a part of this human and make another just like him, only strategically different. So from the rib of the man "the LORD God fashioned a woman" (2:22). When the man sees the finished product, he's elated: "This one finally is bone from my bones / and flesh from my flesh" (2:23).

If there is anything that these two stories tell us about us human beings, it is that we are very, very special, and very, very, very complicated. We're made in the image of God, which is enough to take one's breath away. But we're also a product of the soil, as common as the stuff we scrape from our shoes after walking in the mud. But common as this soil is, it is nevertheless supremely significant because the breath that inhabits it has come from the mouth of God. Human life has a uniquely divine quality. John Donne said, "any man's death diminishes me."[1] This conviction begins with the creation story. Because of what we humans are, any human death, at whatever the point in human existence, is significant to humankind as a whole. That is, life is never *cheap*, since the breath of God is in all of human life.

Our complexity begins, then, with the very way we're made and the very stuff of which we're made. Our pattern is the very God of very God, since we are made in God's image. Later, when the tempter solicits Adam and Eve by suggesting that they can "be like God" (3:5) one wonders why they didn't answer, "Big deal! This is already written into our DNA," or something to that effect. But this "image of God" is only part of the story. In the later nuts-and-bolts description, we're this fascinating combination of common dust and divine breath: "a bit of sod and a breath from God," as I have described it elsewhere. The best topsoil hardly seems an adequate carrier for the breath of God; one might fear that the clay couldn't handle such grandeur. Indeed, perhaps this is part of our problem, that we carry a greatness that tests our equipment. We sense as much at times of our extremity: when we are at our best, closest to God in our adoration of the divine or in our service to others, we may feel that we're about to burst with gladness, love, and beauty. At the opposite, when human creatures declare themselves independent of God, they seem to usurp the breath of God as if it were not a gift and think themselves too good for the clay of which they're made.

Our complexity is still more dramatic in our social incompleteness. Breath of God or not, we need others. The lone human being, as the writer of Genesis describes us, searches for something that can't be found in even the magnificence of nature or in the relationship humans can have with animals. Indeed, we humans can commune with God, but God expresses no jealousy in the fact that this is not enough. We are so made that we are incomplete. One of the most enduring popular songs, "People," says that "people who need people / are the luckiest people in the world." That describes all people, and the need can seem devastating when it goes unfilled. In my years as a pastor, I counseled now and again with lonely people who wanted above all else to have another person in life. We humans are extraordinary creatures, but we're incomplete: we're better off with a rib missing—that is, giving something strategic of ourselves to another—than when we crush what we are to ourselves.

Sometimes we say, "I'm just a simple human being," but in fact there's no such creature. To be human is to be wonderfully complex. We need to be right with nature because we're part of it and we're responsible for it. We long for God because there's a God-shaped void in us which only God can fill. Thus, we keep making gods for ourselves if we don't get at least a rudimentary relationship with God the Creator. And we need others. They may irritate us and frustrate us, and we quite rightly need time away from them at proper intervals ("proper" being defined differently from one person to another). But after all is said and done, we need one another.

But this is only the beginning of the story of our ancestors and of us. When we get one another we also get trouble. We humans have trouble enough managing ourselves. As the noble monk, Godric, says of himself in Frederick Buechner's novel, "Godric's war is all within. For fifty years the only foe he's battled with has been himself."[2] Yet a major part of Godric's battling comes by way of his thoughts about his fellow human creatures. Because when we try to relate our own divided and self-confused personalities with other equally divided and confused persons, we have a highly combustible mixture.

Adam and Eve found it so. And so have all of their descendants, if I may tell you what you already know. We need one another, and we can't really live without one another, but we also make life difficult for one another—sometimes almost unlivable.

Our trouble came with our priceless human ability to make choices, which is something we're programmed to do. The problem, of course, is that the quality of our choices is entirely up to us. One bright, fateful day "the most cunning of all the beasts of the field that the Lord God had made"[3] started a conversation with Adam and Eve. The heart of the serpent's approach was that God didn't really have their best welfare in mind, indeed, that God was jealous of them and had forbidden a particular fruit because if they ate it they would "be like God, knowing good and evil" (3:5).

It's strange that the offer appealed to Adam and Eve. Their setting and lifestyle were so idyllic. Nevertheless, they wanted more. Strange, too, that they were tempted by the appeal to be like God, since they already had such status: they were made in the image of God and blessed with the breath of God. Perhaps, however, they didn't appreciate their own potential; we often don't. Strange, too, that they weren't deterred by the warning that if they ate from the tree they would die. But living in a place where life throbbed on every side, death was unimaginable and unreal.

In any event, they did it. They ate what was forbidden. They used their unique human power of choice to self-destruct. And I suspect this is the point of my subtitle for this particular biography: Adam and Eve are "our kind of people." Fleming Rutledge, the incisive Episcopal clergywoman, puts it this way: "It's clear from the primeval history in Genesis (chapters 1–11) that the human race has been in a self-destructive downward spiral ever since the disobedience of Adam and Eve."[4]

It's been a peculiar spiral. Consider how in some ways we've used our human skills so well: we have all but wiped out several diseases that other generations knew as fatal plagues. It's less than two hundred years ago that human beings could communicate no faster than they could travel; today you or I can talk with someone in any part of the world by telephone or Internet. But our progress is frightfully mixed. Cain killed his brother, but it was in a one-on-one act, as were wars for centuries. Today Cain can kill dozens in a shopping mall or a school, or can in fact drop a bomb that will kill tens of thousands. And while modern communication blesses relationships by its immediacy, it also makes the distribution of lies or pornography equally rapid.

That is, we humans still must exercise our human power of *choice*—and we still need the character to choose well. More than ever, with our increased knowledge and power, our decisions are immeasurably more far-reaching.

Fortunately, our human history doesn't depend solely on us. God has put immeasurable power in our hands and minds, as developments of the past century or two have demonstrated so dramatically. But God hasn't abandoned our human race. If the Bible story were simply the story of Adam and Eve and their descendants, it would descend into a mad tale of the annihilation of the planet and of humanity. But remember, the first Person in the biblical series of biographies is God, and as I noted earlier, God isn't limited to chapter 1.

So it is that when Adam and Eve sinned, God did not forsake them. Neither does God simply wipe them out. In this the tempter was right when he said, "You won't die" (3:4). For one thing, physical death didn't come immediately. Furthermore, God was at hand with a remedy as quickly as the disobedience was committed. How ironic that the tempter—the father of lies!—was truthful in evaluating the character of God. Perhaps it's an instance of the tempter using the truth for untruthful purposes. It isn't the last time that happened.

So God came looking for our ancestors, just as God comes looking for you and me. God asked a question that the humans had to answer: "Where are you?" (3:9). We humans have to acknowledge our spiritual location to ourselves, and to God, if we are to get back on track. God knows our location, but this is incidental to our human story until we ourselves are willing to recognize and confess it.

There were penalties for Adam and Eve. Quite surely, we continue to pay these penalties. This is something of the meaning of Dr. Rutledge's phrase, "the downward spiral." Adam and Eve have children, and when the first, Cain, was born, Eve is ecstatic with hope. But hope turns into bitter tragedy when Cain kills his younger brother, Abel. It looks as if the story could end here. But God responds with grace, giving Adam and Eve another son whom they name Seth. It is significant that when Genesis gives its definitive "record of Adam's descendants" in chapter 5, it says nothing of Cain and Abel. It tells us that when God created humanity, "he made them in the likeness of God," and that when "Adam had lived one hundred and thirty years, he became the father of a son in his likeness, according to his image, and named him Seth," and that after that Adam lived "eight hundred years and he had other sons and daughters" (5:1-4 NRSV). We read earlier that Cain had descendants (indeed, he named a city after his first son). But the plotline comes through Seth, the child of grace.

The Adam and Eve story tells us that what you and I do has consequences for others. Sometimes the consequences appear immediately, sometimes next month, sometimes in the next generation, and almost always—one way or another—for generations to come. And this is true for more than simply our physical descendants. In a profound sense, nothing we humans do is ever altogether private—not even our inmost thoughts. All we do reverberates out and down and up and around. We never live or die simply to ourselves. Adam and Eve tell us as much by their story. And they're our kind of people: wonderful, complicated, God-seekers, God-fleers, the stuff of the earth, and now and then the salt of the earth.

So were Adam and Eve heroes, rogues, or "the rest"? Pretty clearly they were all three. They started as heroes, and they became heroes again in raising Seth. But they were the first of a line of rogues. That's what theologians mean when they speak of our "Adamic nature." It's in this business of their choosing that they got in trouble. Because by their choice they became heroes or rogues.

And like it or not, they're our kind of people.

CHAPTER 3

Abraham and Sarah:
Pioneers of Promise

You may wonder why I make a big leap from the story of
Adam and Eve to that of Abraham and Sarah. Certainly a
good deal happened in the interim. But if we're to tell a story
by way of biographies, we look for those persons on whom the
door of history turns. This is as true of the biblical story as of a
given family, movement, or nation.

To be sure, there are some fascinating persons along the
way, the kind of people that stir the imagination of novelists
and sometimes of preachers. Lamech, for instance. If you begin
with Adam, Lamech is the seventh generation. This could be
significant to an Old Testament scholar because in the Hebrew
Scriptures seven is the number of completeness. We might there-

fore expect something special of Lamech. I hesitate to say that Lamech is *special*, but he *is* memorable. He is the first biblical character to be identified as having multiple wives, and their names are recorded for us. We don't know the name of Cain's wife, or Seth's or Noah's, but we know the names of both of Lamech's wives. And the names are rather telling: Adah means "ornament," and Zillah means "defense."

Lamech's descendants are notable, too: founders of economic and cultural empires. On the dark side, Lamech is a murderer; and worse, he boasts about his murder in a song to his wives. Later, there is Nimrod, "the first great warrior on earth" (10:8). Still later, there were the rebels at Babel who built a tower, saying, "let's make a name for ourselves" (11:3-4)—and ironically, and no doubt significantly, they are anonymous.

Then, on the side of godliness, wonder, and beauty, we have Enoch, who "walked with God" (it's said of him twice [5:22, 24]) and who "disappeared because God took him" (5:24). The New Testament book of Hebrews includes him in its catalog of the heroes of faith (Hebrews 11:5-6). Very few biblical characters with such a short biography have evoked more sermons and more passionate wondering.

As for Noah, if this were a longer book we would surely give him a long chapter. He's a symbol of hope to those who live in any dismal time because at a time when "humanity had become thoroughly evil on the earth and that every idea their minds thought up was always completely evil" (6:5), "Noah was a moral and exemplary man; he walked with God" (6:9). Thus, when it looked as if the human race would simply destroy itself by the weight of its own iniquity, Noah was the greater weight of righteousness. One person's righteousness outweighs a mountain of the rebellions and sins of others! He, too, is in the list of faith heroes in the book of Hebrews (11:7). His life encourages those in any generation of corruption that one godly person can make all the difference.

But the biblical story didn't turn a corner with Noah. It appears that the story wouldn't continue without Noah, and he is surely an enduring hero of goodness. But he is a continuation of the plot rather than a shaper of it. For the shaping, we turn to Abraham and Sarah.

Their entry into the story is altogether routine, by way of one of those genealogies that we tend to despise. "When Terah was 70 years old, he became the father of Abram, Nahor, and Haran" (Genesis 11:26). Then, "Abram and Nahor both married. Abram's wife was Sarai.... Sarai was unable to have children" (11:29-30). Then we read that Abram and Sarai and their orphaned nephew, Lot, led by Abram's father, Terah, "left Ur of the Chaldeans [a major city at the time] for the land of Canaan" (11:31). For some reason, however, they stopped short of Canaan and, in time, Terah died there.

Then the story makes its crucial turn. Both religious and popular history often note that Abraham is the father of the three great monotheistic religions—Judaism, Christianity, and Islam. It all begins sometime after Terah's death, when God calls Abram to leave everything—land, family, and father's household—"for the land that I will show you." There, God promises, "I will make of you a great nation and will bless you. I will make your name respected, and you will be a blessing.

> I will bless those who bless you,
>   those who curse you I will curse;
> all the families of earth
>   will be blessed because of you."
>   (12:1-3)

Centuries later, the writer of the New Testament book of Hebrews praises Abram's faith: "He went out without knowing where he was going" (Hebrews 11:8). The writer of Genesis says, "Abram left just as the LORD told him, and Lot went with him" (12: 4). As these biblical writers report it, Abram said neither yea nor nay; he simply did as he was told. I tell myself that surely he said *something* in the face of such an abrupt call. Thus I respond heartily to Father Kilian McDonnell's poem "The Call of Abraham," when he pictures Abraham talking back to God, upset by God's "imperious" style, arguing against the call to

> place my thin arthritic bones
> upon the road
> to some mumbled nowhere.

But the poem ends with Abraham saying, "You come late, Lord, very late, / but my camels leave in the morning."[1] I empathize with Father McDonnell's interpretation, but I'm fascinated by the way the biblical writers tell the story, by what they include and also by what they choose to omit.

Genesis tells us that Abraham was seventy-five years old at the time of his call, and we learn later that Sarah was just ten years younger. They had been unable to have children, so the promise of a great nation coming from them, and that through them "all the families of earth will be blessed" seems altogether unlikely. They're going without a declared destination except that they're headed for Canaan. This must have sounded quite primitive and uninviting for someone who had established a thriving agro-economic business in Ur and then in Haran. But away Abraham and Sarah went, and the biblical story turns a once-and-for-all corner with their obedience. Fleming Rutledge calls this event "the inaugural moment in the history of redemption."[2] I can't think of a better way to describe it.

They are coleaders in this venture, though Abraham gets most of the best lines. Obviously, however, Sarah is crucial to the story because they are promised a family line, and certainly Sarah is crucial to that goal. Furthermore, while Abraham is a towering figure by any measure, Sarah stands beside him with impressive stature of her own. The New Testament writer recognizes as much by naming her along with Abraham in the list of the faith heroes (Hebrews 11:8-19).

So notice some things about Sarah. Abraham's faith is by way of direct communication from God, while it appears that Sarah's comes via Abraham; that is, it is only many years later that we have any record of God speaking directly to her. Blessed are those who trust God on the basis of what another tells them—which includes many of us at one time or another: the church committee that follows the lead of the pastor, the pastor who trusts the guidance of a bishop or a congregational vote, the spouse who moves on the basis of the thinking of her/ his professional mate. Sarah's pain in leaving "land, family, and father's household" was no less painful than Abraham's, and she did it, as far as we know, without the same divine assurance. She moved on the basis of Abraham's faith. Let's call them both heroes.

When famine forced Abraham and Sarah to move to Egypt, Abraham advised Sarah that when the Egyptians saw her beauty they would kill him so that they might claim her; therefore, she would say that she was Abraham's sister (a statement that was the truth but not the whole truth), "so that they will treat me well for your sake, and I will survive because of you" (Genesis 12:11-13). Sarah cooperated, and it appears that the pharaoh took full advantage of the situation (12:19). One wonders that Sarah didn't suggest to Abraham that if his faith was great enough to leave everything and go to the road, it ought also be great enough that he would tell the truth and leave the results with God. This was an act of great personal sacrifice on Sarah's part and dramatic evidence of her faith not only in God but also in Abraham. Abraham seems somewhat a rogue and Sarah a hero.

Then comes a dark chapter. Ten years had passed since God's call to Abraham, and he and Sarah had not yet conceived. In that culture, Sarah saw herself as a failure. She concluded that she was preventing God's promise from being fulfilled. So she turned to a remedy that was standard in her time and place. A woman's personal maid was seen as an extension of herself. If a woman of position did not conceive, the maid could lie in her stead, and if the union produced a child it was seen legally and practically as the child of the woman, with the maid holding no claim.

So it was at Sarah's urging that Abraham lay with the Egyptian maid, Hagar, and she conceived. At this point some very human elements show up. When Hagar "realized that she was pregnant, she no longer respected her mistress." Sarah, in turn, complained to Abraham, and Abraham took the coward's exit: "Since she's your servant, do whatever you wish to her." Sarah "treated her harshly," and Hagar ran away (16:4-6). But an angel of the Lord "found Hagar at a spring in the desert," and reasoned with her to return to Sarah, and even to "put up with her harsh treatment of you," because in time God would bless her offspring (16:7-9). "Abram was 86 years old when Hagar gave birth to Ishmael for Abram" (16:16). Neither Abraham nor Sarah looks good in this episode.

But God isn't done with them. When Abraham is ninety-nine and Sarah is eighty-nine, God assures them in separate instances that they will still have a child. Abraham answers, "If only you would accept Ishmael!" (17:18), because he loves the boy who is by that time in his teens. Sarah got the reassuring word while she was overhearing a conversation between Abraham and the Lord—which in a sense was how she had gotten most of her information. A practical woman, "Sarah laughed to herself, thinking, I'm no longer able to have children and my husband's old" (18:12), but God knew her thoughts and challenged her: "Is anything too difficult for the LORD?" (18:14).

So Isaac was born, and the tension between Sarah and Hagar increased to a point where Hagar and Ishmael were driven from the camp. Students of the ancient world indicate that the relationship of Sarah and Hagar was not uncommon to the mistress-slave world of that time. Perhaps the best we can say is that we're not in a position to judge—but also to note that the biblical story is not about perfect people or even people who are always admirable, but rather about people that God used, no matter. We should especially rejoice that the Bible is honest in all of its reporting. It's not a document doctored by public relations experts who have set out to impress us. The Bible's greatest characters are real (sometimes frightfully real!) human beings. Heroes and rogues in the same skin.

Whatever his inner struggles—and it's clear that there were many—Abraham was obedient to the limit. It was an obedience that was set in faith. Against all odds, from his call to his death, he believed. Of such persons, as the New Testament writer says, "God isn't ashamed to be called their God—he has prepared a city for them" (Hebrews 11:16). Abraham's greatest test came when Isaac was entering young manhood and God called Abraham to sacrifice him "on one of the mountains that I will show you" (Genesis 22:2). Abraham took the assignment in his usual stubborn faith-obedience. In the language of the New Testament, Abraham figured that if he did so, "God could even raise him from the dead. So in a way he did receive him back from the dead" (Hebrews 11:19).

Many things impress me in the story of Abraham and Sarah. As I've just indicated, I see them as such altogether human personalities, cutting corners in ways that embarrass me and that nevertheless comfort me, since I know a bit about my own humanness. But I am in awe of this. When God called Abraham to leave everything he held dear and sacred, Abraham said not a word: he just did it. And when God told him to put his son Isaac—"your only son whom you love" (Genesis 22:2) as the Lord describes him—Abraham didn't plead his case; simply this, "Abraham got up early in the morning" (22:3) and set out to do what God was telling him to do. The closest Abraham ever came to contesting a point with God was on the occasion when his faith wavered enough, in light of his age, that he would suggest to God, "If only you would accept Ishmael" (17:18).

This was Abraham's attitude toward himself and his own welfare. But once there was a time when Abraham argued a case with God, then pressed it, and pressed it, and pressed it, until he was embarrassed to ask one more time. He did this, not for himself and Sarah, but for his errant nephew, Lot, and for the even more errant community where Lot lived, Sodom and Gomorrah. (Genesis 18). A divine delegation visited Abraham and Sarah to tell them that they would have a son within the year, but then went on to reveal that the two great cities not far away were to be destroyed because, "The cries of injustice from

Sodom and Gomorrah are countless, and their sin is very serious" (18:20).

At this point Abraham begins an appeal on behalf of the two cities and their inhabitants. We assume that Abraham's primary concern is for Lot and his family, but Abraham begins his appeal on ethical grounds: "Will you indeed sweep away the righteous with the wicked?" (18:23 NRSV). Then Abraham became specific, and I suspect he was doing so on the basis of some things he had observed: If there were fifty righteous in the city, would God not forgive it "for the sake of the fifty innocent people in it" (18:24)? Perhaps emboldened by his own words, Abraham suggested that this would be inconsistent with God's nature: "Will the judge of all the earth not act justly?" (18:25).

The dialogue that follows is one of the most remarkable in all of Scripture. Abraham asks for a continually lower standard until he stops with ten: will God spare the cities if there are ten righteous, and God agrees that it will be so. Unfortunately, there aren't even ten, and Sodom and Gomorrah are destroyed.

God had told Abraham and Sarah that through them "all the families of the earth will be blessed" (12:3). As it happens, the blessing cannot cover Sodom and Gomorrah because each soul decides for its own salvation; the faith of another can never be transferred intact to another's benefit. It is also true that if Lot's righteousness had been more effective, perhaps more would have been saved beyond himself and his two daughters.[3]

The continuing human story has its share of Sodom and Gomorrah times, sometimes on the scale of individuals and families and sometimes of generations or nations or eras. Few, if any, are as dramatic and measurable as Sodom and Gomorrah, but the principle holds true: the human story can endure only so much wickedness before evil devours itself. But always there are the spiritual descendants of Abraham and Sarah, the people of faith and works who are a redemptive power in both the worst and the best of times.

I speak of "the people of faith and works" because this is the combination that made Abraham and Sarah so notable. The apostle Paul held up Abraham as the example of faith, reminding us that "Abraham believed God and it was credited to him as righteousness" (Galatians 3:6, Genesis 15:6). But the apostle James is just as pleased to tell us that Abraham was "shown to be righteous through his actions" (James 2:21), and that "faith without actions has no value at all" (2:20). That is, to use a contemporary phrase, Abraham was the complete package: he believed and he acted; he had faith and works.

Fleming Rutledge raises a question in a fine sermon on Abraham: "Why Abraham?" She continues, "The answer is given very simply in the first verse of the twelfth chapter: 'The Lord spoke to Abraham.' Abraham has done nothing whatever to deserve this attention. Abraham is nothing in himself."[4] That is, God had faith in Abraham. I rejoice greatly in this, that God had faith in Abraham.

But then I remind myself of something. God also had faith in Adam and Eve, who were made in God's image. Indeed, God has faith in all of us since we're made in the divine image with the breath of God. But as the story of the Bible unfolds, and your story and mine, the issue is this: it's quite marvelous that God has faith in us. Now will we have faith in God and everyday actions to live out our faith? That's the question as our human story unfolds, this story of heroes and rogues and others.

CHAPTER 4

Jacob and His Kin: The Uses of Dysfunction

As I said earlier, I marvel at the honesty of the Bible. Yes, and more, I rejoice in this honesty, and I wonder why we don't make more of it. That is, I marvel that the Bible never glosses over the failings of its characters or tries to explain and justify their actions. This open reporting includes the heroes, but more than that it seems sometimes to save the sharpest of its candor for those who matter most. The persons who are key to the biblical plot are treated with the most transparency.

I don't want to seem irreverent, but as I read the Scriptures I sometimes feel that God deserves sympathy in his dealings with the human race. When God is patient with the sinner, some complain that God has no standards because anything seems to go—almost as if God doesn't care. When God sends judgment, however, some ask how anyone can worship such a brutal God. No wonder some prefer a deistic view of God, a god who observes the human story from a safe distance. The hands of such a god are never tainted by human mud. Not so with the God of the Bible, who deals with us humans as we are and thus is contaminated by our sins and fumblings.

Nearly a century ago a British writer, William Norman Ewer, pondered in four brief lines:

> How odd
> Of God
> To choose
> The Jews[1]

Well, if it was odd, God had fair warning in the first of the tribe, an agro-business genius named Jacob. The name itself spelled trouble, and he got the name in the peculiar circumstances of his birth. The second of twins, he was gripping the heel of his older brother as he emerged from the womb so they named him "heel-grabber": a name that carried the idea of a supplanter, or even a cheat. Later, God changed Jacob's name to Israel, the name that officially identifies the Jewish people to this day.

Jacob was the grandson of Abraham and Sarah. He had the business smarts of his grandfather, but he also had an ethical code that was sometimes suspiciously flexible, and the Bible does nothing to hide these dealings. He took advantage of the naïve bungling of his older twin brother, Esau. And though he hesitated, he didn't refrain from deceiving his own father, Isaac. It looked as if Jacob had met his match when he went to work for his Uncle Laban. Jacob said of him, "You changed my pay ten times" (Genesis 31:41). It may have been poetic exaggeration, but not much. Nevertheless, when Jacob left his association with Laban, he was "very, very rich: he owned large flocks, female and male servants, camels and donkeys" (30:43).

It was when Jacob left home to escape the justifiable wrath of his brother Esau, that he came to work for his Uncle Laban, and in the process married Laban's two daughters—Leah and Rachel—and later the two concubines who were the the girls' maid servants. Between them these four women blessed Jacob with twelve sons and a daughter. And with it all, a quite dysfunctional family.

It was largely Jacob's fault, of course, but the circumstances were hardly ideal. Jacob adored Rachel, the younger daughter. As a contemporary translation puts it: Rachel "was graceful and beautiful" (Genesis 29:17). But on the wedding night, Jacob's father-in-law, Laban, deceived him, and Jacob awakened the next morning to find that he was married to Leah, a woman apparently poor in comparison with her younger sister in physical attractiveness but admirable for her courage, character, loyalty, and faith. She bore him six sons and his only daughter.

Unfortunately, none of those children, or the four sons born to the concubines, fulfilled Jacob. He wanted a child by his first and probably only love, Rachel. When at last that son, Joseph, was born, Jacob immediately put him above all of the rest. Worse, he made his preference very clear to the older brothers (and a later younger brother, Benjamin) when Joseph was still in what today we would call his midteens.

It was not a pleasant household in which to live. Jacob was brilliant in agro-business but a failure in family psychology. Eventually the ten older sons formed a fairly organized league against Joseph, and when an opportunity came, they disposed of him by selling him to some itinerant traders, telling their father that Joseph must have been eaten by a wild beast, supporting their story by showing their father bloody, doctored evidence in the magnificent coat Jacob had given to Joseph (Genesis 37).

Jacob is a key figure in our unfolding human story, and so is the dysfunctional nature of his family. If there had not been such an enmity between Joseph and his older brothers, they would not have tried to eliminate him. If it hadn't been for some dissension among the brothers, they would probably have simply murdered him. Instead, they sold him into slavery. As it turned out, the slavery had its setting in Egypt, surely the most advanced country in the Middle East at that time. I submit that the family of Jacob would never have become the nation of Israel—a nation that, against all odds, exists to this very day—had Joseph never been sold into slavery in Egypt because it was in Egyptian slavery that the descendants of Jacob were shaped into a people that eventually became a nation.

No matter how the circumstances of life catapulted Joseph into the air, he had a holy gift for falling on his feet and always landing leagues closer to his destination. Joseph succeeded so well as a household slave that he became the most trusted person in the entire staff. This proved to be a precarious position, however, because it brought Joseph into frequent contact with the wife of the owner. She was a woman hungry for attention, and when Joseph tried to resist her approaches he ended up falsely accused. He not only lost his job, he was thrown into prison.

Even in prison, however, Joseph's character and ability stood out. In time (a matter of several years) he was the most trusted of the inmates, serving as a kind of auxiliary to the jail's commander. The Bible puts it this way: "The jail's commander paid no attention to anything under Joseph's supervision, because the Lord was with him and made everything he did successful" (Genesis 39:23).

But to put it in folk language, everything in Joseph's life to this point was small potatoes. In time, in a series of fortuitous circumstances touched with the miraculous, Joseph became second in command to the pharaoh of Egypt. The teenager who was his father's favorite and his siblings' victim, the boy who went from prized employee to a jail "where the king's prisoners were held" (39:20), is now, at thirty years of age, the second most powerful man in the ancient world.

In the plotline that you and I are following, however, Joseph's success is only a means to an end. Because while the story of Joseph, in its barest outline, inspires the reader to steadfast living and to confidence in God's providential care, its much greater significance is its part in the birth of a nation. While Joseph was leading Egypt through a period of unparalleled abundance and then a drought that engulfed both Egypt and surrounding areas in famine, Joseph's father and the extended family moved to Egypt. At the time of their coming they numbered some seventy people, no more than you might find at a healthy family reunion. There were no doubt hundreds if not thousands of such extended families in the Middle East at that time. This one, however, became a nation, the nation of Israel: that is, the people we know today as the Jews. I believe I can safely say that no nation in existence today is as numerically small yet so widely spread over the world and so influential in such a variety of fields. Nor is there a single nation that has endured as much persecution and survived as many campaigns of extinction.

Some of the ugliest words in our human story are related to the suffering of this people. *Ghetto* now means a section of a city where an underprivileged ethnic or racial group is forced to live, but it first meant a section in cities in most European countries where all Jews were required to live. *Pogrom* is now a figure of speech for mass slaughter, but it came into our human vocabulary as "organized massacre, especially of Jews." We once thought of a *holocaust* as vast destruction, especially by fire, but now to mention the word is to think of Adolf Hitler's effort to destroy the entire Jewish people.

What made them such a nation, a people repeatedly victimized through several thousand years of history, yet not only surviving but constantly emerging as leaders? Devout persons in both Judaism and Christianity will say that it is because the Jew is a chosen people to whom God has given a special mission. But what are the human circumstances by which this remarkable story came to pass? How is it that an ancient family of seventy, born to one man and his two wives and two concubines, exists today as an independent ethnic group in essentially every part of the world?

A generation or two after the time of Joseph, the pharaohs of Egypt came to fear the Israelites. The Israelites lived in a separate part of the country and rarely intermarried with persons from outside their clan; indeed, the Egyptians and Jews alike preferred it that way. But the Israelites were multiplying and prospering, so the Egyptians subjected them to national slavery—a life they endured for several hundred years. Such a role will either break the spirit or refine it. In the case of the Israelites, it molded them into a nation. They saw their identity as unique. They were the descendants of Abraham, Isaac, and Jacob, the people of promise, the people through whose descendants the nations of the earth would be blessed. To this day, centuries later, they celebrate their escape from Egypt in the feast of the Passover. Even those who no longer identify themselves as Jews by religion, and some who think of the whole story as a myth, still celebrate the story of a slave nation which, in a legendary past, was delivered from bondage by the hand of God.

There's more to the history of Jacob's family and it centers especially on this issue of dysfunction. The writer of Genesis interrupts the story of Joseph while the young man is en route to Egypt with the trader caravan so he can tell a peculiar, complicated story about Jacob's fourth son, Judah. The story occupies all of Genesis 38, after which the historian returns to the Joseph story. You wonder why the Genesis writer interrupts what appears to be continuing plot at a crucial juncture to tell us, as some novelists used to say, "Meanwhile, back on the farm."

In this case, "back on the farm" is a strange series of events from the life of Judah, a member of the family about whom we've heard nothing except a sentence or two in the discussion about Joseph's fate. We're told that Judah "moved away from his brothers...saw the daughter of a Canaanite whose name was Shua, and married her" (38:1). Their union was blessed in apparently quick succession with three sons: Er, Onan, and Shelah. The oldest son, Er, marries "a woman named Tamar." However, God considered Er "immoral" and "put him to death." Judah then instructed the second son, Onan, to "Go to your brother's wife, do your duty as her brother-in-law, and provide children for your brother" (38:8). This was part of an ancient code among many peoples: if a man died before his wife had conceived a son, his next brother was to marry the widow with the understanding that the first son conceived would bear the name and family line of the deceased; thus a man's family line would continue. Onan didn't like this arrangement, however, so "he wasted his semen on the ground, so he wouldn't give his brother children" (38:9).

As a result, he too was put to death. At this point Judah apparently concluded that Tamar was bad luck. He told her, "Stay as a widow in your father's household until my son Shelah grows up" (38:11). This was of course humiliating for Tamar; a woman didn't return to her father's house once she had married unless there was some unworthiness in her. Obviously Judah hoped Tamar would simply go away so that in time he could give his son Shelah to another woman.

"After a long time" (38:12)—long enough that Shelah had grown up—Judah's wife died. By now Tamar had discerned that she was not in her father-in-law's plans for Shelah, so she took matters in her own able hands. Hearing that her father-in-law was in the area on business, she took off her widow's clothing, "covered herself with a veil, put on makeup, and sat down at the entrance to Enaim on the road to Timnah" (38:14). Tamar had calculated rightly. Judah "thought she was a prostitute because she had covered her face" (38:15); and because he didn't have the price for lying with her, he left a security guarantee: his seal, cord, and staff. When his associate returned to clear the debt, Tamar was gone.

Three months later Judah heard that his daughter-in-law was pregnant. Indignant, he ordered that she be burned. Tamar, however, sent Judah the seal, cord, and staff with the message, "I'm pregnant by the man who owns these things. See if you recognize whose seal, cord, and staff these are" (38:25). Judah admitted his guilt in not giving her his son Shelah in marriage. Twins were born of the union, Perez and Zerah. So it is that dysfunction was carried into another generation, in dramatic and salacious fashion.

Obviously there's a reason why the writer of Genesis included this story—the kind you'd expect a family historian would keep out of the records. As the rest of the Genesis story unfolds, Judah becomes the key figure, the one through whom the plotline develops. Thus, when Jacob (Israel) pronounces final words on his sons before he dies, he speaks the most significant words not for Reuben, his firstborn, nor for Joseph, his favorite son, but for Judah: "Judah, you are the one / your brothers will honor" (49:8), Jacob declares, and he goes on to predict,

> The scepter won't depart from Judah,
>> nor the ruler's staff
>>> from among his banners. (49:10)

Thus, several generations later, when the book of Ruth is reporting on the genealogy that leads up to the iconic King David, it begins the lineage with (of all people!) Perez, son of the union of Judah and his daughter-in-law Tamar. Stranger still, it seems to exalt the story because when the elders of the village congratulate Boaz on his plans to marry Ruth, their good wishes include this line: "And may your household be like the household of Perez, whom Tamar bore to Judah" (Ruth 4:12).

As the rest of the Old Testament story unfolds, David, the second king of Israel, becomes the standard by which all the other kings are judged. If a king is good, it is because he is like David; if he's bad, it is because he falls short of David's standard. How interesting, then, that this revered national figure is introduced to us by his descent from a scandalous union. One would expect that the Jews, a properly proud people, would have omitted this detail from their story. And one would expect that the Bible, a book that aims always for holiness of life and character, would have omitted the story of Genesis 38 in its record—a story that, in fact, seems shoehorned into Genesis.

It's almost as if the Genesis writer is making the most of the dysfunctional quality of Jacob's family. Believe me, there's no virtue in being a sinner. But it's a step toward virtue when we can admit that we're sinners and can move on from there.

Soon after David's grandson, Rehoboam, becomes the king of Israel, the nation divides in a civil insurrection. The ten northern tribes, who take with them the name Israel, disappear from the biblical scene after the invasion by Assyria. We refer to them popularly as "the ten lost tribes." They gradually intermarry with other Middle Eastern peoples. I suspect that today their descendants are part of the complex of Arabic nations. The two southern tribes, plus the tribe of Levi, took to themselves the name of their major tribe—you guessed it, Judah. And it is by a sounding of this name that we know this people today: that is, the Jew.

As for the larger biblical plot, let's jump to the New Testament for just a moment; specifically to its first book, the Gospel of Matthew. That book begins with a genealogy of Jesus Christ. Early in the record it has this data: "Jacob was the father of Judah and his brothers. Judah was the father of Perez and Zerah, whose mother was Tamar" (Matthew 1:2-3). In this passage you see "Judah and his brothers" with the eleven brothers (including even Joseph) as unnamed supporting cast. You also see a special line for Tamar, who is one of only four women (including Mary) mentioned in the lineage of our Lord.

And this Jesus is, of course, the Savior of the world. How remarkable, how unlikely, that the story should have a major turn with Jacob (himself unlikely enough) and his dysfunctional family! Heroes, rogues, and the rest? Indeed. And sometimes it's hard to tell which guy is wearing which hat.

CHAPTER 5

Moses: Freedom to Obey

When we paused in our biographical journey (including a brief New Testament stop in the Gospel of Matthew), Jacob's family was becoming slaves in Egypt. That doesn't seem an auspicious setting for a sparkling future, but it will prove to be just that.

This slavery lasted for several centuries. It probably began in relatively moderate form and then increased in restrictions and severity until it reached the kind of inhumanity where any form of human subjection is likely eventually to lead. It extended over enough years—generations—that the Israelites could have lost all sense of their worth. They went from being an isolated people (a role they seemed to accept without objection) to becoming despised. Perhaps the worst power in any form of human suffering, whether ill health, poverty, or physical or political oppression, is that in time it can break the human spirit. A person—or a people or a nation—can be so accustomed to their pain or deprivation that they see it as their rightful state in life. Thus, persons who suffer one sickness after another often come to feel that sickness is the norm for them. So, too, with generations of poverty or enforced inferiority. If for generations you and your people have known only bondage and despising, you can hardly imagine any other way of life.

Somehow, however, the people of Israel—the descendants of Jacob—maintained a sense of significant identity. Was it the phrase, "the people of Abraham, Isaac, and Jacob," that kept them going? Did they pass from one generation to another the conviction that God had called their ancestors and that they were to be an instrument of blessing to all the earth? We can speculate as a poet or a political dreamer would do, or we can seek to brush the idea aside in tough-minded common sense. One way or another, however, this people managed to cherish their identity and to feel their separateness as a people. And as I've indicated earlier, slavery added to their sense of being a people of unique identity held together partly by their common suffering. Somehow, too, elements of faith and character remained in this otherwise downtrodden people. They were down, held down under the heel of their oppressors, yet they maintained some sense of community worth. They were down, but they refused to be out.

It's at this point that Moses enters our story.

Moses is not only a key biographical figure in the biblical story of our human destiny, he is at the same time one of the towering personalities of music, poetry, drama, and legend. Americans who read this book have closer ties to Moses than most of us realize. Contemporary American writer Bruce Feiler suggests that "Moses was America's true founding father." Feiler makes his point in winsome, compelling fashion, as he follows American history from the Mayflower—when the leader, William Bradford, compared their journey with that of Moses and the people of Israel "when they went out of Egypt"—all the way to the twenty-first century.[1]

But Feiler notes that the connection began even before the Mayflower. When Columbus set sail for the new world, he compared himself to Moses. The Moses connection gained power in succeeding generations. Thomas Paine was seen by many of his contemporaries as a religious pagan, but he was enough of a student of the Scriptures to compare King George III to Pharaoh, and of course that identification keys in on Moses. The Moses story is made-to-order for the issue of slavery, which is the major crisis of American history after the nation's founding. One of the most notable and poignant of the spirituals is "Go down, Moses." The oppressed who sang it for generations drew an eloquent picture in a few words:

> Go down, Moses,
> Way down in Egypt land.
> Tell old Pharaoh,
> "Let my people go!"

And of course there are endless stories of slaves in the Civil War period who referred to President Lincoln as their Moses.

Mr. Feiler notes also that Presidents Woodrow Wilson, Franklin Roosevelt, and Lyndon Johnson employed Moses's name in wartime. Those familiar with biblical language will always remember that Martin Luther King Jr. drew upon the

Moses story in his last public statement on the night before his assassination, in words that took on an eerily prophetic quality.

But even if Moses's name and words didn't appear in America's political speechmaking, his presence is inescapable in the nation's capital. There is a Moses statue in the Library of Congress. In the chamber of the house of Congress, the face of Moses appears among twenty-three figures who undergird the principles of American law, but Moses's place is unique: eleven of the bas-relief figures face left and eleven face right, and all look toward Moses; and as Feiler notes, his is the only one shown full-figured.[2] There are six representations of Moses in the Supreme Court of the United States. A stranger to the United States and its history might conclude, after a tourist's trip through Washington, DC, that Moses was one of our founding fathers along with Washington, Adams, and Jefferson.

Moses's prominence in the American story is fascinating for those who live in the United States and, for that matter, to persons in nations coming to birth in any part of the world. But it isn't the heart of our story. From a biblical point of view Moses is not only a liberator of an enslaved people, a leader who managed to hold together a people who had no understanding of freedom and its limits, or a great lawgiver. Beyond all of that, the Bible sees Moses as the one who officiated at the covenant between God and the people of Israel. In that role, he symbolizes God's desire for a committed, continuing relationship with our whole human race.

Moses's story is in a class by itself. It begins at a time when the leadership in Egypt was becoming increasingly nervous because of the growing population of the Israelites. They had come to Egypt as an extended family, but now—as the Egyptians saw it—they were "larger in number and stronger" than the

Egyptians (Exodus 1:9). I doubt that they were stronger, since the Egyptians had the advantage of an armed military. But established peoples are always uneasy when they see another, alien community becoming powerful in its own right.

So they put the Israelites into the kind of labor where they could "harass them with hard work," building storage cities for Pharaoh (1:11). Nevertheless, the Israelites continued to multiply. Eventually, Pharaoh ordered that all baby boys born to the Hebrews should be thrown into the Nile River. One Hebrew couple, however, saw their son as especially "healthy and beautiful," so they risked their lives to hide him for three months. But it's hard to hide a healthy baby for long. So the mother, assisted by the baby's older sister, placed the infant in a small, tarred basket and trusted the tiny human cargo to the reeds along the riverbank of the Nile.

There the baby was found by the best and most unlikely person: the daughter of the Pharaoh who had ordered the male infanticide. Her response was that of a woman with maternal instincts rather than those of an indulgent princess. She adopted the child as her own, naming him Moses, "because...I pulled him out of the water" (2:10). It was an appropriate name not only because it described how she had rescued the child but also because it described how he would someday rescue his people from slavery and past the waters of the Red Sea.

So the unregistered alien grew up in a setting that an early Christian, the martyr Stephen, would describe centuries later this way: "Moses learned everything Egyptian wisdom had to offer, and he was a man of powerful words and deeds" (Acts 7:22). The best thing about Moses, however, is this: the luxury of the palace and the excitement of expansive learning did not make him forget who he was. "One day, after Moses had become an adult he went out among his people and he saw their forced labor. He saw an Egyptian beating a Hebrew, one of his own people" (Exodus 2:11). Ordinarily, we humans accept advantages and benefits as our due. An instinct for justice generally needs nurture. One marvels that a man who had lived with benefits, isolated from the sufferings of his people and probably trained to think that what the government of the palace did was of course right, would instead react with a sense of justice. What he did—murder a particular oppressor—was not right, but the instinct for justice that drove him was nothing short of astonishing.

But this meant that the adopted son of privilege became an international fugitive. Moses spent the next forty years herding sheep for the father-in-law he gained in the land of Midian. What does a scholar learn while tending sheep? What does a child of privilege learn in a role of essential destitution? Enough that one day when God called him from "a flame of fire in the middle of a bush...[that] didn't burn up" (3:2) he was sure that he could not fulfill the divine assignment. As we have just noted, the New Testament writer saw Moses as a man who had "learned everything Egyptian wisdom had to offer," but he saw himself as a man with "a slow mouth and a thick tongue" (4:10). Ironically, however, Moses was quite forceful, perhaps even eloquent, when it came to arguing with God.

Who can say, ultimately, what makes someone a leader? How is it that a nineteenth-century slave, like Frederick Douglass, could become a personality of such power that his opponents would put a price on his head? Or that Franklin Delano Roosevelt, a man so crippled by polio that he couldn't rise to his feet without help, could lead a nation through a cataclysmic depression and a world war?

Moses ran from the assignment and gave in only when he was allowed to have his brother, Aaron, as his coleader—an arrangement that proved questionable on more than one occasion. Moses and Aaron got off to a good start. When they told the Israelite elders and then the larger body of the people that "the LORD had seen their oppression, they bowed down and worshipped" (4:31). But the first flush of enthusiasm died quickly. When Pharaoh responded to Moses and Aaron by enforcing tougher, more inhumane working conditions for the Israelites, the people told Moses, "You've made us stink in the opinion of Pharaoh and his servants. You've given them a reason to kill us" (5:21).

It's not surprising that Moses then complained to God, "Why did you send me for this? ... You've done absolutely nothing to rescue your people" (5:22).

It was a long and difficult negotiation between Moses and Pharaoh. There were plagues and more plagues, negotiations, and promises and broken promises before, at last, Pharaoh not only let the Israelites go, but he ordered them to leave. Then he changed his mind again and pursued them to the dramatic end at the Red Sea, where a miracle occurred that should have convinced Israel once and for all that God was on their side. But even miracles are easily forgotten when people run into adversity, and Israel got a full quota of adversity. Each time things went badly, or threatened to do so, the people rebelled against Moses. He led the people for roughly forty years, and it was only as the nation stood at the edge of its journey, and Moses was at the end of his life, that the people gave him a sustained vote of confidence.

By that time I doubt that Moses felt any need of vindication. He had stared down Pharaoh, so to speak; he had led the people through trackless wilderness and the edge of hostile nations; he had seen them through times when they seemed ready to die of thirst along with frequent grumbling about their diet. He survived a crucial failure in leadership by his brother, Aaron, when Aaron was left in charge of the nation for a time, as well as several revolts, including one led by his sister, Miriam, and Aaron.

Worst of all, there was a time when it seemed that even God had given up on the whole enterprise. It happened in this way. When Moses was on Mount Sinai, receiving the ten commandments and the essential document of agreement between God and Israel, the people "saw that Moses was taking a long time to come down from the mountain. They gathered around Aaron and said to him, 'Come on! Make us gods who can lead us. As for this man Moses who brought us up out of the land of Egypt, we don't have a clue what has happened to him'" (32:1).

Aaron didn't hesitate. He didn't seek a straw poll or attempt to negotiate or to stall for time. Instead, he took up an offering of gold rings and earrings from the people and made an image of a bull calf. The people declared, "These are your gods, Israel, who brought you up out of the land of Egypt!" (32:4). Aaron took this as a satisfactory plebiscite and "built an altar in front of the calf" (32:5).

We humans often demonstrate short memories, but this demonstration is classic. We humans often rebel against those who have served us well—whether parents, teachers, or dedicated public servants—but certainly there have been few if any rebellions to compare with this one. When Moses saw what had happened, he "was furious." He broke the tablets of the law that God had given him in the sacred precincts of Sinai, shattering them into pieces—appropriately, because his nation had broken the law by their conduct even before the law was fully received.

He then burned the golden calf, ground it into powder, "scattered it on the water, and made the Israelites drink it" (32:20). This man who told God at the time of his call that he had "a slow mouth and a thick tongue" (4:10) certainly shows no signs at this point of any such limitation.

But the people, difficult and irresponsible as they were, were now the lesser half of Moses's problem. Moses found himself at odds with God even before speaking so forcefully to the people. "I've been watching this people," God said, "and I've seen how stubborn they are. Now leave me alone! Let my fury burn and devour them. Then I'll make a great nation out of you" (32:9-10).

If I may say so, it had to be a tempting offer. Not that it appealed to Moses's ego; I'm no judge of that matter. But Moses could well have reasoned that almost anyone would be better than the thankless crew he had worked with for those several years. No matter! Moses now reasoned with God. He reminded God that God had invested "great power and amazing force" in bringing these people out of Egypt. What would the Egyptians think if they heard that God had now wiped them off the earth? Then Moses reminded God who these people were: "your own people." Then, especially, Moses referred God back to the covenant itself—a covenant that had begun with Abraham, Isaac, and Israel—with its promise: "I'll make your descendants as many as the stars in the sky. And I've promised to give your descendants this whole land to possess for all time." The sacred historian said that "the Lord changed his mind about the terrible things he said he would do to his people" (32:11-14).

Moses wasn't done. When the crude and dramatic day drew to its close, Moses reaffirmed where he stood. "But now, please forgive their sin! And if not, then wipe me out of your scroll that you've written" (32:32). God answered, in effect, that it was his business as to who was saved and who was not. But Moses had made one of the grandest statements this side of Calvary. He had declared that he cherished his people (and he knew better than anyone what a fickle, disloyal, easily misled group they could be) more than he cherished his own soul and his ultimate relationship to the Lord God. And with it all he challenged God to demonstrate the character that Moses was sure God possessed.

You and I live in a time when the very term *leadership* has received a reverence in the world of business, politics, sports, and religion. Books on leadership easily find a place in the bestseller lists of publishing. One wonders how many ways lessons in leadership can be dressed in new garb or whether, perhaps, the whole concept is simply a case of the emperor's new suit. So, too, with lectures on leadership; apparently we can't get our fill of them. So what shall we say about a leader called Moses, who could transform a family of freed slaves into a nation and hold them together, homeless, for a generation, victorious over the ravages of body, mind, and spirit?

Two pictures stand out in Moses's gallery. For one, "the man Moses was humble, more so than anyone on earth" (Numbers 12:3). Our contemporary culture doesn't often associate humility with leadership; we think instead of a leader as confident, self-assertive, and take-charge. But perhaps we're drawing our images from would-be leaders rather than lasting ones, and perhaps also we don't realize the quiet strength that comes with humility. Moses's special gift of humility was this: that he saw his mission as more important than his person. His importance was in the work he was called to do. I suspect all of the true and lasting leaders of human history have been persons of this disposition. This fits the shorthand description of the difference between a politician and a statesman; politicians are concerned with the next election—that is, themselves—while statesman are concerned with the next generation—that is, their nation, state, or municipality.

Then, there's the concluding summary of Moses's life and character in Deuteronomy: "Moses knew the LORD face-to-face!" (34:10). The biblical writer explains this unique distinction by contrasting it with the matters that otherwise seem so important: "That's not even to mention all those signs and wonders that the Lord sent Moses to do in Egypt—to Pharaoh, to all his servants, and to his entire land—as well as all the extraordinary power that Moses displayed before Israel's own eyes!" (34:10-12). Moses had pleaded with God that he might see him face to face. It was a continuing revelation. He saw God in the darkness of his own failure when he murdered the Egyptian taskmaster and in the apparent purposelessness of ten thousand days of tending flocks in the desert and then being apprehended by a burning bush. He saw God in failed attempts with Pharaoh and in his own apparent failures in leading Israel.

But there was more, far more. He saw God in forty days on Sinai, so far from human beings and so near to God. And then, perhaps above all, Moses dared to stare into the eye of what appeared to be the wrath of God and ask God to reconsider. At this point of blasphemous audacity he was supremely humble. He made himself utterly dispensable if only the purposes of God and of the people of God could be fulfilled and that the character of God could be affirmed.

In the process, the biblical writer dares also to portray God not only in human language but also in flawed terms in order to make his points about the relationship between God and humanity. Don't press the details of the story too logically; just be grateful that the biblical writers take us into territory that stretches our souls. And thank God that there was once a baby in a basket, a shepherd at a bush, a man arguing with God—a man called Moses. We couldn't have the story without him.

He was a hero, for sure, and he was helped by some heroes, too, like Joshua and Caleb. And there were rogues: Pharaoh, brutal taskmasters, even Aaron, and others who challenged Moses's leadership. At times, even God seemed to take the rogue role. But the purposes of God go on, and the plot continues to unfold, even against impossible odds. And Moses stands tall, head bowed under the weight of leadership, but soul high in trust.

CHAPTER 6

Samuel: The Purposes of Government

When we think of Samuel we think of a miracle baby or a serving boy in a temple. I'm sorry that our thoughts so often stop there, because the lovely story of Samuel's conception and the story of his boyhood encounter with God are only preludes to the far more significant events in his adult life. We understand the early stories best when we see them as preparation for the unique genius that follows. Samuel is the transition figure in the governing of the Old Testament people, Israel. Without him it's hard to imagine how the people of Israel would have established a political identity that would last.

Let's begin Samuel's story where the Bible does, in a confused household with two wives. One wife was deeply loved whereas the other was successfully productive. Theirs was a culture where the productive—the good fortune to conceive children— mattered more than any other consideration. For some years, the barren woman struggled with what she saw as her hopeless failure. Then she pressed God for a miracle and got it: a son, the boy Samuel. She had promised God that if she gained a son she would give the child back to God to serve in the temple. And so she did.

The boy grew up in a singular setting because his mentor, Eli, was both the spiritual and the political head of the nation. It was a nation badly in need. The biblical writer puts it succinctly: "The Lord's word was rare at that time, and visions weren't widely known" (1 Samuel 3:1). Thus, when God first called Samuel, Samuel had no idea that it was God even though in his growing up he "was more and more liked by both the Lord and the people" (2:26). Eli was pretty much a failure as father to his own two sons; nevertheless, his knowledge of God and his walk with God were enough that he was able to counsel Samuel on the night of Samuel's divine visitation. He advised Samuel that the voice he was hearing was perhaps the voice of God, and he told Samuel how to respond. So it was that the boy Samuel began a career like no other, a career in which he led his people, Israel, from the uncertain, Wild-West days of the books of Judges and Ruth into a relatively established empire with structures of continuing leadership. Samuel is a lesson in the purposes of government, and he has a unique place in the story we're following.

It isn't a neat, tidy story, but if you've ever had anything to do with government or politics, you know better than to expect the story to be neat and tidy. In fact, the events that set the stage for Samuel's leadership are messy and tragic. As I've already said,

Samuel's mentor, Eli, apparently failed badly as a father. His sons used their inherited position to steal from the people and to seduce women who came to worship. A nation with such corruption at the top is doomed to collapse eventually. For Israel it came in a war with their traditional enemy, the Philistines. Israel tried to guarantee victory by taking into battle the sacred chest that symbolized their divine relationship. They were sincere, but with the kind of sincerity that reduces true faith to magic and superstition. Not only did the Philistines rout Israel's army, they captured the sacred ark of the covenant. Both of Eli's sons were killed in the battle. When the word reached Eli, he fell over backward in shock, and the fall broke his neck, taking his life. His daughter-in-law, great with child, went into labor and gave birth to a son. She died just after the birth, naming her son "The glory is gone" or "Where is the glory?" It sounded more like the epitaph for a nation than the name for a child, which is apparently just what she meant it to be.

The biblical writer tells us nothing of what Samuel did in the years that followed. It's clear that he became the spiritual and political leader of the people, but we don't know what he did in the years after Israel's defeat by the Philistines. We know only that "a long time passed—a total of twenty years...and the whole house of Israel yearned for the LORD" (7:2). We know, too, that Samuel had come to have such standing with the people that he dared to challenge the nation. It was not a feel-good speech. If you're in earnest, he told the people, "get rid of all the foreign gods.... Set your heart on the LORD! Worship him only" (7:3). The people responded to Samuel, and the nation entered a period of peace and prosperity.

The time came when Samuel, in advanced age, appointed his sons to take over his position of leadership. At this point,

Samuel's story takes an ironic turn. His sons "didn't follow in his footsteps. They tried to turn a profit, they accepted bribes, and they perverted justice" (8:3). That is, they did pretty much what Eli's sons had done in their generation. One wonders how Samuel could have allowed such conduct after what he had seen of Eli and his sons. I'm afraid we human beings are slow to learn, sometimes even when we have presided over the same lessons when they applied to others. And of course it's quite possible that Samuel did what many a busy, successful parent has done: became so involved in running the nation that he neglected his own family. We have so many examples of this sort of parental failure that you'd think we would learn.

In Samuel's case, the failure brought more than personal pain and something more far-reaching than the military defeat that followed Eli's failures. When the sons of Eli failed, young Samuel gradually moved in to provide spiritual and political leadership. With the failure of Samuel's sons, however, no spiritual successor was standing in the wings. Furthermore, the people had become disillusioned with the system as they had experienced it with both Eli and Samuel. So a delegation of Israel's elders came to Samuel's headquarters. Their message was direct: "Listen. You are old now, and your sons don't follow in your footsteps. So appoint us a king to judge us like all the other nations have" (8:5).

Did you catch it, that telling phrase? "a king...like all the other nations have." Nations get jealous just as individuals do, which isn't surprising since nations are made up of individuals. We don't have enough data about ancient Israel and their neighbors to compare their conditions, so we don't know why Israel would think they'd be better off with "a king like all the other nations have." I suspect it's the kind of comparing all of us are susceptible to, the feeling that life is better in the other person's yard. Contemporary novelist Jerome Charyn says that the first book of Samuel is "the history of a tribe that has become tone-deaf. The Hebrews have forgotten how to listen."[1] It's a fair description not only of Israel in Samuel's time, but of a variety of nations in the course of human history, and also of individuals—again and again.

Samuel was a great soul. We wouldn't include him in this study of the major characters in the biblical story unless he had unique credentials. But like every other great soul, he was utterly human, and as in other instances, the Bible doesn't hide his lapses of greatness. Samuel felt, with reason, that the people were rejecting him. More than that, he felt that they were rejecting the form of government he represented. God consoled Samuel in his failure, insisting that the people were rejecting God, not Samuel, and that this conduct should not surprise Samuel because Israel had been doing this sort of thing, God said, "from the day I brought them out of Egypt to this very minute, abandoning me and worshipping other gods" (8:8).

God wasn't going to abandon Israel in return. Rather, God told Samuel to "comply with their request, but give them a clear warning, telling them how the king will rule over them and operate" (8:9). Samuel seemed to relish the second part of this assignment. He was graphic and specific in telling the people what it would be like to have a king. The elders of Israel were unmoved; they just wanted to "be like all the other nations" (8:20).

When the king was introduced, it looked as if Israel had struck gold. Saul was the son of a wealthy farmer. In a nation that was almost entirely agricultural this meant that Saul was one of the people, but one of the more successful. Furthermore, as the

Samuel

Bible record puts it, "No one in Israel was more handsome than Saul, and he stood head and shoulders above everyone else" (9:2). But best of all, Saul seemed to have a remarkable store of natural humility. When Samuel approached him, Saul protested that he was from Israel's smallest tribe, which was true, and that he came from the "littlest of the families in the tribe," which seems like humility beyond the facts (9:21). But it's clear that Saul didn't desire grandeur. When the time came for Samuel to present him to the people as their king, Saul was hiding among the supplies. Furthermore, when the first call came for his military leadership, the messengers found Saul back on the farm, keeping the cattle.

Everything about Saul was appealing. He wasn't impressed with himself. He was a person with great personal attractiveness—what today the media would call charisma—but he seemed unconscious of his gift. If anything, he seemed to run from the favors and accoutrements of his office.

So we're saddened and surprised by what followed. Saul began shortly to overreach, assuming rights that were not his and that presumed upon his relationship with God and with the boundaries of his office. One senses early that he was jealous of his own admirable son, Jonathan. In general, he was assertive and protective of his office. Many of his actions suggested insecurity. Perhaps then it isn't surprising that on an occasion when the prophet Samuel came looking for him, he learned that Saul had gone to Carmel "where he is setting up a monument for himself" (15:12). When we're insecure we build monuments of one kind or another to impress others with our importance but far more to convince ourselves of an importance we're not sure we have. So it was that Saul began to crave more power, more praise, and more attention. It would be helpful if we could develop a test to indicate how a person might react to the embellishments of power before being chosen to be president of a nation or of a corporation, chair of a committee, or pastor of a church. No potion intoxicates as quickly as power or has such an increasing appetite for still more of the same.

Saul's story always makes me very sad. Jerome Charyn says that Saul "haunts us like no other character in the Bible.... He's the very idea of the king as a lonely man."[2] I can't help feeling that in many ways Saul was a good man, and certainly a person with much potential. I don't see him as a mistake. I see him, rather, as what I've seen in many persons whose potential was good but who couldn't handle the burden of success. Not many fall as publicly and dramatically as Saul, but many have a biography written with essentially the same outline.

So God called Samuel to anoint a successor. This is a strange story. Saul was still in office, and he would continue so for a number of years. But his successor had to be divinely authorized and this was a job for Samuel, the prophet of God. So Samuel anointed the shepherd boy, David, but apparently no one knew of David's appointment—no one, that is, but David himself. David received this presumptive anointing when he was still tending sheep, apparently last and least in his family as the eighth son in a family of boys.

It's clear that David never played on the role that would eventually be his. On one occasion a very perceptive woman, Abigail, protected him from a fit of umbrage that could have spoiled his career before it began to mature. Twice he had made-to-order opportunities to kill Saul, but he refused on principle and religious conviction. David seemed to understand that the throne should come to him by God's direct action, not by his manipulation.

Samuel was long gone when David finally became king, but Samuel's mystical presence hovers over the story. David ascended to the throne by steps, serving for seven years over only his own tribe, Judah, and then for thirty-three years over the united nation. He enjoyed unparalleled military and political success. As the biblical writer puts it, "The LORD gave David victory wherever he went" (2 Samuel 8:6). But while he won victories on the battlefield, in the halls of government, and in the records of civil historians, he stumbled badly as a husband, a father, and a man, and those failures hurt his kingship.

Nevertheless, the Old Testament writers saw David as the model king and his reign as the measure for all who followed him to the throne. If a king was good, the biblical historian had a word for it: "He did what was right in the LORD's eyes, and walked in the ways of his ancestor David" (2 Kings 22:2). God's standard for someone ruling over the people was that such a person would do "what was right in the LORD's eyes," and if the king wanted that standard to be translated into an example he would find it "in the ways of his ancestor David."

Unfortunately, as one king followed another, those who received the award of excellence were few. In the time of David's grandson, King Rehoboam, the nation of Israel divided; ten of the tribes followed Jeroboam and held to the name Israel, and the remaining tribes took the name of Judah, the dominant tribe. Within a relatively short time, as history measures it, the ten tribes of Israel disappeared. Specifically, the Assyrians conquered them and took the best of them captive, leaving only a minority to watch over the land. In time, these Israelites intermarried. They are lost to us today. We often refer to them as "the lost tribes of Israel." They are lost just as many ethnic groups have been lost over the centuries through intermarriage with the dominant people.

The people in the southern kingdom, Judah, continue to this day. We speak of them as the Jews, a vocalization, so to speak, of their national name, Judah. Judah, too, was taken captive; in their instance, by Babylon. But they survived their captivity. One may well wonder why Judah survived as a nation even without a country of their own, while the larger body disappeared. Many factors played a part, but I'm impressed by this one: that from time to time Judah had a good and godly king, while no king of the ten northern tribes ever received such an appraisal. Both nations had prophets who declared God's word to them; the quality of their land was generally equal. They were of the same basic ethnic stock as descendants of Jacob. No doubt several factors were at work because history is never simple. But I can't escape the difference I've just mentioned, that intermittently Judah had good kings, a favor the northern tribes never enjoyed. Government makes a difference.

What kind of government should it be? Hereditary kings? Dictators? Oligarchy? Democracy? When Samuel was a boy, Israel was ruled by judges, part-time leaders who served as both the judicial and executive branches of government as we know it today. Reference is sometimes made to the elders of the tribes, who probably served in an informal way—as a kind of legislative or advisory body, though we have no description of their office or power. When the people asked for a king, Samuel warned them that a king would take their sons to serve in his army; their daughters to be his perfumers, cooks, and bakers; their best fields for himself; and a tenth of their grain and their vineyards (1 Samuel 8:11-18).

Samuel saw the nation through transition from judges to a system of hereditary kings. It's interesting, however, that a certain kind of democracy was at work. When the people came to Samuel and asked to have a king, God said to Samuel, "Comply with the people's request—everything they ask of you—because they haven't rejected you. No, they have rejected me as king over them" (8:7). That is, God had chosen and empowered Samuel, so when the people asked for a king, they were rejecting God as well as Samuel. But I'm intrigued by the order, "Comply with the people's request." Democracy indeed.

I like democracy. A democratic society is the only kind in which I've ever lived, and I'm not looking for any other. Indeed, my concern these days is that we're losing the power of the people to a variety of interest groups—economic, political, and social.

So what kind of government does the Bible recommend? A government where we "do justice...love kindness...and walk humbly with our God" (Micah 6:8 NRSV). That is, a way of life where those who have been blessed with the most will seek to bless those who have less, and where people will use power and advantage to protect the rights of even the least. In truth, there is of course no perfect government since our governments work with imperfect people. We can hardly expect absolute justice, mercy, kindness, and integrity as long as there are so many who want inevitably to use government, whatever its form, for their own ends. And all of us are more susceptible to this evil than we realize.

So back to our question: What kind of government do I hope for? Well, the kind of government that will happen when God's will is done on earth as it is in heaven. This, ultimately, is what Samuel wanted but which he couldn't manage even with his own sons. It is what the great Hebrew prophets constantly called for. It is what Jesus talked about when he called for the kingdom of heaven. And it's what you and I pray for each time we pray for God's kingdom to come on earth as it is in heaven. I intend to keep praying for it. I will try—always inadequately—to work toward it. And I will remember that what Samuel oversaw in painful transitions that never fully fulfilled God's purposes, the writer of Revelation envisioned as happening some triumphant day in the City of God. Of this I am sure: this is what God wants, so I am confident that it will someday happen. It is my privilege and yours to work, pray, and believe to that blessed end.

CHAPTER 7

David: The Importance of Singing What You Think

S ome years ago I wrote a devotional book that led its readers through the Bible, Genesis to Revelation, with a devotional reading expositing the Scripture portion for each day.[1]
My aim was to help persons read the Bible in the usual order
of the biblical books so they would get the continuing plot of
the Scriptures. I made one exception, however, to the pattern of
reading. At irregular but rather frequent intervals through the
year I inserted chapters from Psalms and Proverbs.

I did this for several reasons, but primarily because these
books, with their 181 chapters, don't advance the plot of the
biblical story. Psalms and Proverbs are books of worship and
wisdom, respectively, and they are written in the form of Hebrew

poetry. Job, Ecclesiastes, and Song of Songs (or Solomon) are also books of wisdom written in poetic form, but they had enough of a "plot" within themselves to fit into the general scheme of the book.

But even if Psalms and Proverbs don't fit into the plot, the Bible would in no way be complete without them. In truth, I suspect that a great many people know the Bible primarily for one or both of these books because of the comfort they find in the Psalms and the insights for living in the Proverbs.

More than that, however, the Psalms and Proverbs weave their way through the plot in all the rest of the Bible. A faithful Bible reader feels the influence of these books even while reading the rest of the story. It's as if they give a melody to the plot, and perhaps a harmony too. We understand the creation story in Genesis better if at some point we read what the psalmist says about the creation (for instance, Psalms 8, 19, and 104). So, too, with the stories of the people of Israel, as in Psalms 44 and 105–7. You see the wisdom of Proverbs shaping events in other parts of the story and influencing a New Testament book, James. Psalms and Proverbs are part of the rest of the story, whether quoted or not, just as background music advances the plot of a movie, often without our even realizing that it's doing so—sometimes, in fact, without our even realizing that music is playing.

It is significant that roughly half of the Psalms are attributed to David, Israel's greatest king, and that Ecclesiastes, the Song of Songs, and much of the book of Proverbs are popularly seen as the work of King Solomon, David's son. Some feel that these attributions were made to honor David and Solomon or perhaps to lend more authority to the writings. That's possible, and I understand the scholarly reasoning behind such thinking. But whether one accepts David and Solomon as the original authors or credits the authorship to them as an honor, the point is the same: the Bible connects Israel's two primary kings with poetry and music and wisdom. The Bible invites us to remember David and Solomon not only as regal administrators—or in David's case, as a military genius—but also as men of worship and of literary instincts. We picture David with his harp or Solomon pondering life's wisdom as he strolls through his palace gardens. But more about that later.

Let's look for a time at biblical poetry and wisdom. Hebrew poetry is unlike poetry as we usually think of it, that is, as writing marked by rhythm and often also by rhyme. Hebrew poetry has rhythm, and most Bible translations in the last half century demonstrate this by the way they lay out the lines of the poetic books and the poetic portions of other books. But the primary sense of rhythm in biblical poetry is the rhythm of *sense*. We call this *parallelism*: the practice of two or sometimes three lines making the same point, as if to say, "Once is not enough."

Hebrew poetry doesn't do this simply by repeating the same words, as in what we currently speak of as "praise choruses." Rather, they reinforce a point by saying it another way. For instance, "The heavens are telling the glory of God; / and the firmament proclaims his handiwork" (Psalm 19:1 NRSV). Sometimes the parallels are longer and more complex:

> Do not remember the sins of my youth
>   or my transgressions;
> according to your steadfast love
>   remember me,
> for your goodness' sake, O LORD!
>   (25:7 NRSV)

The principle is the rhythm of sense. The examples I've just given do this in *synonymous* form: the same thought expressed in essentially the same way, just as synonymous words convey essentially the same meaning but with a slightly different emphasis or a particular nuance.

Sometimes Hebrew poetry accomplishes this same end by parallel lines that are *antithetical*; that is, lines that make the same point by way of contrast. For example, Psalm 1 ends this way: "for the LORD watches over the way of the righteous, / but the way of the wicked will perish." The point is that it's better to be righteous, and the poet makes the point by contrast—antithesis. This form of parallelism appears often in the book of Proverbs: "The fear of the LORD is the beginning of knowledge; / fools despise wisdom and instruction" (Proverbs 1:7 NRSV).

There is a third common form of biblical poetry. I call it *complementary* because it completes a thought, but students more often use the word *synthetic*, in that it synthesizes a thought. Thus, "I cry aloud to the LORD, / and he answers me from his holy hill" (Psalm 3:4 NRSV), or "I was glad when they said to me, / 'Let us go to the house of the LORD!'" (122:1 NRSV).

The Psalms were meant for worship, both public and private. As C. S. Lewis said, they were "intended to be sung; not doctrinal treatises, nor even sermons."[2] It's good to remember that, as Mary Ellen Chase wrote a generation or more ago, "the predominant element of all music in ancient Israel was rhythm, not harmony, and that melody as we know it today held a very subordinate place."[3] Some of these psalms are so clearly for the whole congregation that one can almost hear a body of people singing them, while others are so private that we seem to intrude as we listen in. Nevertheless, there come times when these private psalms are so appropriate to our own state of life and soul

70

that we know they belong to us as surely as they belong to the persons who originally wrote them.

The book of Proverbs (and also Ecclesiastes) is wisdom literature. Ancient cultures honored wisdom in ways that I think we can hardly imagine today, and surely no ancient people honored wisdom more than did Israel. For them, wisdom was not just a human gift or attainment, but a divine gift. Proverbs isn't satisfied to exalt wisdom, it despises foolishness. Thus, the book of Proverbs uses several nouns where we would be satisfied with simply the word *fool*. The Hebrew word that can be translated as "simpleton" was used to describe someone who was weak and thus easily led astray. But this person is not beyond hope. Somewhat worse is the person described as "one who had no sense" (Proverbs 7:7), the kind of person Shakespeare called a "lack-brain." Some translations call such a person "void of understanding," or "without sense."

For some "fools" the Hebrew language (and the book of Proverbs) uses a still stronger word, one that describes a coarse and hardened person, the kind who boast of their folly. This is the word Proverbs uses in 26:11: "Like a dog that returns to its vomit, / so a fool repeats foolish mistakes." Such a person wouldn't be persuaded even by a hundred stripes (17:10). Still worse, in the usage in the Proverbs, is the word *scorner*. John Paterson, the twentieth-century British biblical scholar, said that in such persons "There is something of the highbrow...his folly savors of arrogant superiority."[4] It's impossible to reason with persons who think themselves superior to everyone else. But the worst of all, in the Hebrew collection of fools, was the "fool by name and the fool by nature. He is the churl who calls white black and black white. He inverts the scheme of moral values...totally lacking in ethical and spiritual perception."[5]

As I ponder what I've just written, I remind myself that biblical Hebrew is sparse in its use of words, with ten thousand words where the Greek has two hundred thousand and modern English something like a million. How fascinating, then, that the Hebrew has so many words to describe the person who lacks wisdom or who in fact despises it! This is because the Hebrews saw wisdom as a moral virtue. The wise person was not simply clever or possessing accumulated knowledge, but someone who was righteous. Mind you, the Proverbs are highly practical; they have much more to do with the daily business of living than with philosophical concepts. But for the biblical writers, the ultimate test was a good and circumspect life. The twentieth-century American writer Conrad Richter titled his novel *A Simple Honorable Man* about a back-country Lutheran pastor. The Hebrews would agree with "honorable," but they would have seen this person not as simple, but as admirably wise, with the wisdom that shows itself in purity of life, thought, and conduct.

But back to my earlier point. You can't tell the Bible story—and indeed, you can't tell the human story—without talking about music and the lyrics that go with music, which is in some form or other poetry. And as I suggested, I think it significant that Israel's two most memorable kings are also credited with authoring poetry. "David is like a musical score," Jerome Charyn writes. "He 'civilizes' the Hebrew with his lyre."[6] It is a playful sentence but it's also an analysis of David's remarkable gifts as man, poet, and leader. Later, as Charyn compares Saul—the failed king—and David, he says of Saul, "He lacks David's sense of politics and song."[7]

I'm not entirely sure what Charyn means, and I don't want to twist his meanings to my purposes. Nevertheless, it sounds like the thing I'm trying to say: there is in the biblical story this connection between the wisdom of poetry and the gift of effective leadership. Perhaps someone should write a book about leadership—whether in politics, business, or sports—to see the connection between the poet and the leader. One might also wonder if there are some leaders who should have concentrated on poetry, and some poets who might better have gone into politics.

So David is remembered by his people and by the Scriptures as a poet, a man who sang to God about his dreams, his days of loneliness, his sense of sin, and his gratitude in times of preservation and triumph. The songs of David reflect the spirit of a nation. Israel knew itself primarily as the people of God. They were a political entity, yes, and more so than ever after they had a king, "like the other nations." They engaged in warfare (we wish there were less!), and they had a strict sense, as described often in their songs, of responsibility to those who were oppressed or who had little of this world's resources. Their conduct and their decisions in times and occasions may sometimes have contradicted that calling, but their songs always compelled them to remember who they were and of their obligation to live accordingly.

Furthermore, their songs possess the strategic balance of the biblical faith, in the biblical understanding that true godly living is both personal and social. Thus the poet speaks naturally about life's personal struggles, and just as naturally about the nation's fidelity or lack thereof. So David prays,

> How long, you people,
>   will my reputation be insulted?
> How long will you continue

to love what is worthless
and go after lies?
Know this: the Lord takes
personal care of the faithful.
The Lord will hear me
when I cry out to him.

(Psalm 4:2-3)

But another psalm complains to God as a citizen:

We have heard it, God, with our own
ears;
our ancestors told us about it;
about the deeds you did in their days,
in days long past.
. . . .
But now you've rejected and humiliated
us,
You no longer accompany our armies.
You make us retreat from the enemy;
our adversaries plunder us.
You've handed us over
like sheep for the butchering;
you've scattered us among the nations.

(44:1, 9-10)

This is a God who accepts the song of an individual person whose reputation is under attack just as readily as the song of a nation when it is retreating before its enemies.

So these were the songs of a nation, expressing their historic faith as an ethnic body but also declaring the personal faith of individual members of that body. Perhaps the closest experience for an American is an Independence Day event when the audience joins the orchestra or chorus in singing patriotic songs of their nation, then in singing sentimental or romantic songs that reflect the life of persons in the audience that seem typical of their experience as Americans. The difference for the Hebrews, however, is that the songs in the Psalms were essentially their only songs, and they were songs that centered on their relationship with God. No doubt they had other songs, but these songs endured and became the songs of the nation. As such, they shaped the character and faith of the nation even as the songs shaped them. Our contemporary culture is such that we have very few songs that can be said to shape the people of our nation all across the various ethnic, religious, and cultural backgrounds—to say nothing of the age differentials. The Psalms, however, belonged to all the people. Young or old, rich or poor, the people owned the Psalms and the Psalms owned them.

So, too, with the books of wisdom. They became the philosophical base on which God's people lived and moved and had their being. The book of Job made clear that a person's prosperity or distress did not necessarily reflect their standing before God. Ecclesiastes followed the obsessive, long-term ennui of a man who seemed to have everything and who found that it wasn't enough. The book of Proverbs covered every imaginable element in daily living: from how to resist the voice of the harlot to how to prepare for dining with a king. The counsel in Proverbs is as down-to-earth as one might ever hope to find. It sounds not like the counsel of a student of philosophy, but like the kind of thing your grandmother or great-grandmother used to tell you. In fact, it's quite likely that those relatives were quoting adaptations of the Proverbs if not the Proverbs themselves.

But whatever the subject, whether grand or petty, profound or routine, the biblical advisor was working one consistent theme: "Wisdom begins with the fear of the Lord" (Proverbs 1:7 NRSV). And yes, anyone who thinks otherwise is a bit of a fool.

This is the literature of the books of poetry and of wisdom. Its poetic form makes it easy to remember—or to put it another way, somewhat harder to forget. These books are not a compilation of laws; we have that in the Torah, the Pentateuch. Nor are these books documents of history, though it's fascinating while reading the Psalms to relate some of them to particular times in the lives of individuals or the history of the nation. These books do not specifically advance the plot of the grand story of God's relationship to our human race. But they lend a light and insight to that story that we simply couldn't get in any other way. Because the songs of a nation and the writings that reflect its basic standards of conduct tell us very clearly what kind of people constitute a nation or what kind of people they ought to be. These books tell us that Israel was, above all else, a people who belonged to God and that no matter how often they violated that relationship, it was nevertheless the essence of who they were and what they expected of themselves. I repeat: it was not only what God expected of them but also what they expected of themselves.

No wonder, then, that so many of these writings are associated with Israel's two most notable kings, David and Solomon. Israel not only perceived itself as God's people, with the responsibility to lead the nations to a knowledge of God and righteousness, but they saw their legendary leaders as the persons who embodied those standards.

In the midst of their national ups and downs, they remembered who they were via their music; specifically King David's music. Thus when the sacred historian reports on the redemptive leadership of King Jehoash and the priest Jehoiada, he notes that the occasion was marked "with rejoicing and singing, just as David had ordered" (2 Chronicles 23:18). Several generations later another good king, Hezekiah, led Judah in a renewal of faith. The chronicler is more detailed this time: "Hezekiah had the Levites stand in the LORD's temple with cymbals, harps, and zithers, just as the LORD had ordered through David, the king's seer Gad, and the prophet Nathan." When the burned offering was laid on the altar, "the Levites took their places holding David's instruments, and the priests their trumpets." At a crucial point in the worship, "as they began to offer the entirely burned offering, the LORD's song also began, accompanied by the trumpets and the other instruments of Israel's King David" (2 Chronicles 29:25-27).

And the venue was song. Other nations might glory in statecraft or in philosophy. Israel *sang* its story, its convictions, its fears and hopes and dreams. As individuals and as a nation, they sang what they thought and they sought to live up to their singing. We speak of the City of David, Jerusalem. Modern Israel honors David by its flag, the Star of David. But millions of times every day, in hundreds of tongues, people speak the words attributed to David and the poetic wisdom attributed to Solomon. Human history keeps unfolding, and we play the story by way of lyrics and melody. The songs of Israel and its wisdom have become the impetus for God's people in the church.

And yes, beyond, because untold persons of little or no religious conviction quote the music and wisdom of Israel. Without knowing it, they take the language of Scriptures they may never have read and accept it as their mood and, in a measure, their guide. They endorse the importance of singing what you think.

CHAPTER 8

Elijah: Voices in the Wilderness

If history is biography, who are the main actors? The dates we memorized in history classes would suggest that generals shape history via our wars because those dates stay with us. Or political leaders have done so via their reigns, revolutions, uprisings, and elections. And sometimes documents do as well, as with the Declaration of Independence or the Magna Carta and, of course, the Ten Commandments.

And then there are *voices*. Sometimes they come our way from positions of power so that we hear them because of their platform; nowadays we refer to such instances as the "bully pulpit." But some have no such visible support, and we listen to them simply because we can't do otherwise. In some instances, tyrants or mobs (that is, companies of little tyrants) silence these voices by imprisonment or death. Even then, such voices often continue to be heard. Sometimes these voices have come on city streets, as with Jonah at Nineveh, and sometimes on a commanding mountain, as with Amos. Often, however, these voices came right into the palaces of kings and queens as the word of the Lord to the rulers of the people.

But whatever the geographical setting, they were voices in the wilderness. I speak of the voices of the prophets of God, and these prophets spoke best in the wilderness of human rebellion and wandering. God is always on the search for our human race, and the prophets led the way. John Paterson describes the Hebrew prophets as "unique and without parallel." Where other cultures had soothsayers and seers, the prophets of Israel were not "bound by magic and mechanical technique"; rather, they were an insistent voice for personal and national morality. As a result, they have given us "words the world has not been willing to let die."[1]

The prophets are as mixed a company as you could hope to find. There are dozens of them, ranging from someone like Micaiah, a great soul who comes to us only in a passing story, to Isaiah, whose words continue to be quoted millennia later by people in politics, literature, and human reform. Some of these persons may care little about religion but they love the majestic language of Isaiah. Over a period of several centuries there were probably hundreds of prophets doing their work in their respective regions. We know that there were schools of the prophets, where young men prepared for the office, though we have no record of any of the graduates ever contributing to the prophetic heritage. But it's altogether likely that for every prophet whose inspired word is preserved for us in the Old Testament, there might have been a dozen or a score who spoke into the darkness of their own time and place and to audiences that were perhaps small and apparently inconsequential.

They were a very special people, no doubt about that. After all, the writings of those we call the literary prophets make up a substantial portion of the Hebrew Scriptures; page-wise, over a quarter of the Old Testament. So why have I chosen Elijah, who left no book bearing his name, to represent this divine calling?

Elijah was a prophet who confronted a particularly wicked king and queen and who preached in a time of consummate spiritual decline. Though he left us no books, his few words and deeds are dramatic and memorable enough to inspire an oratorio that has captured audiences for nearly 170 years. He seems to have symbolized the prophetic ministry to the Jews. Thus, when John the Baptist appeared people wondered at first if he was the Messiah and, learning that he was not, they asked, "Then who are you? Are you Elijah?" (John 1:21). They asked this because it was commonly understood that before the Messiah came, the prophet Elijah would reappear to prepare the way. Indeed, when Jesus took his three key disciples—Peter, James, and John—to "the top of a very high mountain, where they were alone" and where Jesus was transformed before their eyes, "Elijah and Moses appeared and were talking with Jesus" (Mark 9:2, 4).

This was a graphic way of saying that the Hebrew Scriptures endorsed Jesus because Moses and Elijah represented "the Law and the prophets," a phrase that symbolized the Hebrew Scriptures just as we sometimes refer to the Bible as, "from Genesis to Revelation." Elijah was, so to speak, the embodiment of the prophetic tradition. He was the voice of God, calling the people of God back to their spiritual roots. The Hebrew prophets were never the founders of a new religion or of an offshoot of Judaism; rather, they called the people back to their original role. More often than not, they did so when the nation was in a spiritual and moral wilderness.

The prophets as a whole were iconic figures, the kind that novelists might love to capture or that could fascinate an astute movie maker, but Elijah was the very essence of their calling and ministry. He appears on the biblical scene without introduction or background information. A reader might easily think that a paragraph had been omitted. The biblical historian is telling us that a new king, Ahab, has come to the throne, and gives us a summary of his reign: he "did evil in the LORD's eyes, more than anyone who preceded him." In fact, "Ahab found it easy" to sin like the worst of his ancestors. The writer offers two dramatic for-instances: "He married Jezebel the daughter of Ethbaal, who was the king of the Sidonians. He served and worshipped Baal" (1 Kings 16:30-31). Then, in what the biblical writer feels needs no segue, he writes, "Elijah from Tishbe, who was one of the settlers in Gilead, said to Ahab, 'As surely as the LORD lives, Israel's God, the one I serve, there will be neither dew nor rain these years unless I say so'" (1 Kings 17:1). Mind you, as the Bible was originally written there were no chapter divisions. Thus the unannounced appearance of Elijah is all the more breathtaking. It leaves it to us to make a connection: with someone as bad as Ahab and Jezebel, we need someone as uniquely confrontational as Elijah. No other introduction is necessary.

From that time on, Elijah dominates the scene. That's hard to do when Queen Jezebel plays the female lead because she's a scene-stealer in her own right. Even in our biblically illiterate age Jezebel remains a figure of speech to describe, shall we say, "a certain kind of woman." Nor is Elijah overshadowed by his successor, Elisha, even though Elisha prayed that he might have twice Elijah's spirit, and apparently got it.

In a word, if there is a prophetic icon, it is Elijah. Not in the content of his writing because, as we've already noted, he is not one of the literary prophets. Rather, it is in the way he filled the office of the prophet. He not only preached to kings, he put them in their place: he reminded them that there is God, and that while earthly kings come and go, God remains. He was utterly fearless. To him, a showdown was not a challenge but a privilege. Nevertheless, in some ways he was the most fragile of men. Thus centuries later the New Testament writer, James, would say of Elijah that he "was a person just like us" (James 5:17). Perhaps this is a key to at least something of the prophetic genius, that the prophet is made of the most common clay, with some elements of both gold and iron mixed in.

The prophets appeared because they were needed. God's people, Israel, had a structured religious culture, with priests, a place of worship, and a retinue of associates—Levites—who carried out not only the everyday business of religion but also its several annual feast days. But Israel also needed freelance voices, persons from outside the priesthood (though one of the greatest prophets, Ezekiel, was also a priest). The priests and Levites had hereditary posts; those who belonged to the tribe of Levi knew from birth that they would be part of the religious establishment. Not so with the prophets. They could come from anywhere and everywhere. Nor did they have a term of office. God conscripted them into service at times of particular spiritual need, and when the worst of the conflict was over, the prophets returned to their former occupations.

They came from a wide variety of backgrounds. We know with certainty of only a few. Ezekiel, as I've said, was also a priest. Isaiah was something of an aristocrat; some scholars feel he was at some time a member of the king's council. Amos, on the other hand, was "one of the shepherds of Tekoa" (Amos 1:1), who also identified himself as "a trimmer of sycamore trees" when he was called to be a prophet (7:14). As for Elijah, I sometimes get the feeling that God called him from an ancient gymnasium where he was training future pugilists. But of the majority we know little or nothing of the work they were doing when God called them or to which they returned when their season as a prophet had ended. Probably only a few of the prophets spent a significant period of their adult lives in that calling.

There were both male and female prophets. There are no prophetic books attributed to women, which isn't surprising considering the nature of the times. In a sense, it's remarkable enough that that long-ago culture was spiritually sensitive enough to recognize the word of the Lord whether it came through a man or a woman, and for that matter, regardless of any other judgments or prejudices. Huldah the prophetess must have had exceptionally high standing in her time, in the days of King Josiah. When the high priest, Hilkiah, found a scroll of the Law in the temple, he turned it over to Shaphan, a priestly secretary for reading, who then reported the finding to the king. The king ordered a royal delegation of five men to ask the Lord "on behalf of all Judah concerning the contents of this scroll" (2 Kings 22:13). They, in turn, went to see Huldah the prophetess. She proceeded, in a message of perhaps two hundred words, to bring a word from "the LORD, Israel's God" (22:15). This is the only message we have from the prophet Huldah, but it is enough to let us know the high regard in which she was held by king and court and priests. And although her message was short, it came at a crucial time in the history of her nation's relationship to God and thus to the unfolding eternal plot with which our story is concerned.

It's interesting, too, to remember that when Joseph and Mary brought the infant Jesus to the temple for the act of ritual cleansing one of the two persons who recognized his divine place was the "prophet Anna...[who] began to praise God and to speak about Jesus to everyone who was looking forward to the redemption of Jerusalem" (Luke 2:36, 38).

Nearly all of the Old Testament prophetic books begin by listing the kings who reigned during the term of the prophet's ministry. This is a way of dating the prophet, just as today we may speak of something happening in George W. Bush's second term in the presidency or of something in British history happening in the Victorian era. But it also underlines the fact that the Old Testament prophets spoke to the kings and that they were called to influence the nation's history. Biblical morality was meant to start with the nation's leadership.

Some kings were marginally religious at best. King Zedekiah brought the prophet Jeremiah from the cistern to which he had banished him to ask Jeremiah secretly, "Is there a word from the LORD?" (Jeremiah 37:17). By contrast, good King Hezekiah kept the prophet Isaiah close at hand for frequent counsel. The prophet Nathan dared under God's order to confront King David at the time of his sin with Bathsheba.

Directly or indirectly, the prophets ministered to all the people. The ultimate goal was to keep the chosen people true to their calling. It was because of this calling that God had a continuing argument with their misconduct. Sometimes the prophetic message was to direct the people away from false gods, the gods of the nations around them, but more often the prophet's message was simply a thunderous command to righteous living. Thus, early in Isaiah's message he cries,

> Zion [the poetic name for Jerusalem, the capital], will be redeemed by justice,
>> and those who change their lives
>> by righteousness.
>
> (Isaiah 1:27)

But while Israel and Judah, the people of God, were the particular focus of the prophets, they spoke at times to the surrounding nations as well. The prophecies of Amos began with brief messages to Damascus, Gaza, Ashdod, Tyre, Edom, Ammon, and Moab before speaking to Judah and at much greater length to Israel. When Jonah preached in Nineveh, word got to the king so that even he put on the sackcloth and ashes of repentance. Daniel's ministry was at a time when his own nation no longer had a king, and his unique ministry was to the kings of Babylon and Persia.

All of which reminds us that the word of God is to all people. The Old Testament concentrates on Israel and Judah and the New Testament on the church, but the point always is that the people of God—the Jews and the church—are to lead all nations and all peoples to the Lord God. The holiness of Israel in the Old Testament and of the church in the New is never an end in itself. The goal is that righteousness and justice shall cover all the earth.

When you and I hear the word *prophet*, we tend to think of someone who makes predictions, the sort of person the sports pages refer to as "prognosticators." Without a doubt the prophets did at times predict. Sometimes it seems as if they were speaking with double vision, with their attention on some immediate issue or person while at the same time looking toward a happening centuries in the future. But most of what the prophets declared was a call to righteousness rather than a prediction of future events. Those messages are every bit as pertinent and demanding today as when the prophets spoke twenty-five centuries ago. As for prediction, someone has said that sometimes the prophets hoped that they would be wrong. That is, as they warned of coming judgment it was with a longing that the people would repent so that the predicted judgment would never occur.

Christians come to the Advent and Lenten seasons with a particular bond to the Old Testament prophets. Some seventeen centuries ago Jerome, who translated the Bible into common Latin for his time, said that the prophet Isaiah "should be called an evangelist rather than a prophet because he describes all the mysteries of Christ and the church so clearly that you would think he is composing a history of what has already happened rather than prophesying about what is to come." Many thousands of Christmas cards hail the coming of the Prince of Peace without the senders realizing that they are quoting the prophet Isaiah from six centuries before the birth of our Lord. At the Christmas season we remember that when the wise men inquired in Jerusalem about the coming king, the Jewish scholars turned to the prophet Micah to explain that he would be born in Bethlehem (Matthew 2:3-6; Micah 5:2). During Holy Week, the climaxing time of Lent, we hear readings from chapter 53 of the prophet Isaiah.

The vision of the Hebrew prophets goes beyond even the birth and death of our Lord, however. They envisioned a perfect time, but in the wonderful honesty of the Scriptures they recognized that such perfection would not come easily. Thus Isaiah declared that one day a ruler would come "from the stump of Jesse"—that is, from the line of David—who

> will strike the violent
> with the rod of his mouth;
> by the breath of his lips
> he will kill the wicked,

for this is a ruler whose reign will be marked by righteousness and faithfulness. And in that day

> The wolf will live with the lamb,
> and the leopard will lie down
> with the young goat;
> the calf and the young lion
> will feed together,
> and a little child will lead them.
> . . . .
> They won't harm or destroy
> anywhere on my holy mountain.
> The earth will surely be filled
> with the knowledge of the LORD,
> just as the water covers the sea.
> (Isaiah 11:1-9)

This was the vision of the prophet so long ago. It is the vision Jesus endorsed as he preached about the kingdom of God and instructed his disciples to pray for this kingdom to come, a way of life where the will of God is done on earth even as it is in heaven.

So it is that for hundreds of years the prophets struggled to bring God's people back to their calling and, in the process, to remind them that God's vision for our world is a vision beautiful beyond our imagining. Their message comes to us still today, insisting on lives of righteousness that will counteract the monstrous evil that continues to exist among us.

Elijah was a man of the wilderness in his time, a man who hid by the Cherith Brook, where he was fed for a time by the ravens, and who dwelled in caves in one of the trying periods of his life. So, too, with John the Baptist centuries later, who "appeared in the desert of Judea" (Matthew 3:1). But whether on the streets of Nineveh with Jonah, the palace of the king with Isaiah, or the wilderness of the desert with John, the prophets were always voices in the wilderness. Whatever the times, they dared to locate themselves in God's calendar. Whatever the passing standards of morality and holiness, they spoke from and for an unchanging standard. They railed against poverty that grinds the poor and wealth that makes the rich insensitive. If they were among us today, they would shake their heads at our measures of success as demonstrated in the sports, entertainment, and business stories present in the press and on television and the Internet because they knew only one measure of success: right living before a righteous God.

Such thinking, talking, and writing knows that our world has wilderness hazards until the kingdom of heaven has come. Since this is true, we will always need the voice of the prophet.

CHAPTER 9

Peter, James, and John: Bringing in the Kingdom

Compared to the dramatic Hebrew prophets, the persons who pick up the sacred plotline in the New Testament seem rather tame. Artists have given us images in stained glass, oil, and watercolor, as well as a fair number of statues and engravings, but only occasionally do the apostles come through in such dramatic proportions as do Ezekiel, Daniel, Amos, or Elijah, whether in their messages or activities. Except for the Day of Pentecost, it sometimes seems that the twelve whom Christ chose to be with him were notable mainly for the instances where they were inadequate.

Yet these twelve men have a unique place in the biblical plot. Their number itself is so significant that when one of them, Judas, fell by the wayside, the believers were quick to prayerfully select a successor in Mathias. And when the book of Revelation, at the close of the New Testament, describes the holy city, it is a place with twelve gates bearing the names of the twelve tribes of Israel, and twelve foundations named for the twelve apostles (Revelation 21:12, 14). That is, as the Bible sees it these twelve persons are the continuation and the counterpart of the story that begins with Abraham and Sarah. The promise with which God called Abraham and Sarah, that through them "all the families of the earth will be blessed" (Genesis 12:2), is a promise that moved toward its fulfillment through an assorted group of fishermen, small businessmen, and less-defined young devotees that we call the twelve apostles.

Having said all of that, I really don't want to minimize the quality of the apostles, and it would be blasphemous of me to play fast and loose with their roles. Jesus chose them because they were the most qualified persons available. They fit our Lord's purposes. Except for legends and traditions, we know little about what these men accomplished after the death and resurrection of our Lord, but there is no doubt a basis of truth in these legends and traditions. Only Peter and John receive attention after the four Gospels; it could be, however, that even the most obscure worked miracles of faith and conversion wherever they may have been. When I read of Paul's travels in the closing chapters of Acts, I'm impressed that wherever he went he found believers. Who knows which apostle or which follower of a given apostle established these many churches. Tradition says that Andrew carried the gospel to what is now Scotland, Thomas to India, and perhaps James the Less to Persia, to name just a few.

Certainly one of the most important things to remember is this: no matter how extraordinary particular leaders may be, no leader has succeeded without a supporting cast of what we sometimes call the spear-carriers, those persons who seem disposable and whose work is often ordinary and quite forgettable but without whom there simply wouldn't be any leaders. Indeed, the very term *leader* presupposes a company of *followers*. And the person who neglects these followers or who forgets their importance rather soon ceases to be a leader.

So who were these twelve men? Justin Martyr wrote of them roughly a century later, "From Jerusalem, men, twelve in number, went out into the world; and although unlearned and without talent of speech, they have, through the power of God, made the whole race of men to understand that they have been sent out by Christ to teach the word of God to all."[1]

Almost certainly they were all young. James and John were just getting a start in their father's fishing business. Some say that John was probably still in his late teens. Jesus himself was probably thirty years old when he called the disciples. Since Matthew was a tax collector and thus, in the Roman system, a possessor of what we would today call a business franchise, he might have been the oldest of the twelve. Even so, he would likely have been in his midthirties. While estimating these ages, however, we should remind ourselves that life expectancy in the first-century Roman world was far different from ours today, and that women entered the process of engagement that led to marriage while they were in their early teens and were likely to bear their first child at fifteen or even less. And of course a Jewish boy was considered a man at twelve or thirteen.

There was very little ethnic diversity in the twelve. Eleven of them came from Galilee. Thus when Jesus was on trial, some of the onlookers identified Peter as one of Jesus's followers saying, "You must be one of them, because you are also a Galilean" (Mark 14:70). Only Judas, who came from Kerioth (thus his name, Iscariot), in Judea, was not a Galilean. That nearly all of the apostles came from one small state, no larger than many counties in America, reminds us that these first followers were hardly a cosmopolitan group. If we accept tradition, however, we believe that many or most of them became world travelers, so to speak, and we marvel at it. They took seriously Jesus's command to go into all the world with the gospel.

It's interesting, too, that in this small band of twelve we have at least two sets of brothers: Andrew and Simon Peter, and James and John. At times this must have made for tension in such a small group. It surely did when James and John began envisioning themselves as the persons at Jesus's right and left at the anticipated coming of the kingdom (Mark 10:35-45). If Andrew had been more like his brother Simon Peter, the tension would have been even greater. Whatever the reasons, it is strange that there should have been these teams of brothers in so small a group and that the group learned to live with this built-in potential for strife.

What kind of education or specific preparation did these twelve bring to their calling? If they were to be the cornerstones of a new kingdom, what was their training? Our first inclination is to say that they spent three years in intensive graduate school with Jesus as their teacher, and ultimately, this is the important answer. But what was their undergraduate training, if I may use that term? What did they know before Jesus called them?

The four fishermen were what we would today call "small business people," like the people who run a mom-and-pop store, or the man or woman who has a one-person beauty parlor or barber shop. So, too, with Matthew and his tax-collecting franchise. Simon the Zealot was probably a fairly adept political organizer, the kind of person who might today be a community chief or county operative for a political party or a movement within a party

But what formal education might the apostles have had? Modernity and post modernity, tend to think that education and progress are recent virtues. In truth, support and pursuit of education have had their ebb and flow through history. In first-century Palestine, the world of the disciples, there were schools in every town in Palestine and compulsory education for all children above six years old. In the Jewish home there was education about the ceremonies of the Sabbath and the faith festivals, and each child was taught a passage of Scripture containing the same letters as his or her Hebrew name. Children began very early to memorize psalms. One tractate of the Talmud said it was unlawful to live in a place where there was no school. Education up to ten years of age was exclusively in the Hebrew Scriptures (the Old Testament), beginning with the book of Leviticus.[2] Therefore, while in the judgment of the learned elders and legal experts in Jerusalem, the disciples were "uneducated and ordinary men" (Acts 4:13 NRSV), but they were far from illiterate.

I also like to leave room for natural giftedness. I remind myself that while the American presidency has included some remarkable scholars, beginning with John Adams and Thomas Jefferson, it has had no more brilliant writer than Abraham Lincoln, who had virtually no formal education. Come to think of it, he got his taste for phrase-making where the disciples did, from the Psalms and the prophets of the Old Testament—plus, for Lincoln, the New Testament as well. We underestimate the human mind if we judge learnedness and creativity exclusively by postmodern standards.

What impresses me most about the twelve is the evidence that they were seekers. They were already on the quest for truth, for godliness, for better living when Jesus came into their lives. James, John, Philip, Andrew, and Peter were all followers of John the Baptist before they became Jesus's disciples. Since John was the forerunner of Jesus, the one "preparing the way" for his coming, these five men had a good preparatory course before Jesus laid claim upon them. They must have been earnest seekers after truth to take time from their careers to seek out John the Baptist and to attend his teaching. I venture that a great many of us come to the deeper places in our faith by circuitous routes, many of them not as direct as the path from John to Jesus.

Personally, I would also place Simon the Zealot among the seekers. He comes by a less-predictable route, however. We're not surprised when people come to Jesus via John the Baptist. Neither should we be overly surprised when a person begins the journey in the world of politics and reform and moves on to godliness. Just as true Christianity awakens compassion for those who have not; so, too, persons who are concerned for the downtrodden and underprivileged may find that it is only a short step to the Christ who sought out the "weary and heavy-laden" (Matthew 11:28).

Simon was a Zealot, an ultrapatriotic, intensely religious body. Josephus described the zealots as having "an inviolable attachment to liberty," a people who felt that God was their only Ruler. Some of them became violent radicals, and in some instances assassins. Almost surely Simon must have been attracted at first by Jesus's appeal, "Repent, for the kingdom of heaven is at hand." Simon, too, wanted God's kingdom to come, and in that spirit moved from being a political zealot to a disciple of Jesus Christ.

We don't know the paths by which others became early followers of Jesus and from there were chosen to be part of his twelve. The reason may have been as diverse as we would get today if we were to ask twelve earnest Christians how it is that they first came to Christ.

As all of us know, one of the twelve, Judas Iscariot, betrayed his Lord. It's ironic that more people know the name of Judas as a disciple than recognize the names of James the Less, or Nathanael, or even Andrew. It has become popular to picture Judas as a well-intentioned traitor, a man who hoped that he would force Jesus to action by a showdown with the Jewish authorities. The Gospel of John doesn't encourage that kind of thinking when it tells us that Judas was "a thief. He carried the money bag and would take what was in it" (John 12:6). But however one looks at Judas, his story is altogether tragic. And when I think a bit longer about our human frailty, I'm surprised that only one of the twelve failed completely. Few deny Jesus completely, but many of us do so by drawing to the rear of his followers then slowly dropping by life's wayside. Discipleship is not for the half-hearted.

So I look with amazement on these twelve persons. Substantial crowds had begun to follow Jesus by the time Jesus selected them. Luke tells us that "Jesus went out to the mountain to pray, and he prayed to God all night long. At daybreak, he called together his disciples. He chose twelve of them whom he called apostles" (Luke 6:12-13). We don't know how many disciples Jesus "called together" before selecting these twelve. We don't know if those who were not chosen later became part of the seventy, or whether they simply went back to their previous lives. We do know, however, that Jesus "prayed to God all night long" before making his choices.

We know also that eleven of them were still with Jesus on the night when he was arrested, tried, humiliated, beaten, and sentenced to death. We know, too, that under this pressure they all forsook him and fled, but nevertheless they kept hoping and remained together during the days following his resurrection and ascension, and we know that they were part of the Day of Pentecost. And from there they found their places in Christ's mission to the whole world. Tradition and legend tell us that they went in every direction and that all of them were martyrs except John, who died in old age after a period of imprisonment on the Isle of Patmos.

And we know that the disciples were successful. The fact that I am writing this book and that you are now reading it is prima facie evidence that they succeeded. They were the beginning, and two millennia later hundreds of millions of us name Jesus as our Lord, so obviously they succeeded.

How is it that they did so? I've titled this chapter for three men—Peter, James, and John—because they were the most obvious of the twelve. Jesus himself identified these three as standing out above the others. It's ironic, however, that it is by their standing out that we see how imperfect they were. Peter is notorious for speaking up when he might better be silent and for denying his Lord three times in a style almost as dramatic as his declaration that Jesus was the Christ of God. James and John were the "sons of thunder" who wanted to call down destruction on people who disagreed with them and who jockeyed for positions of prominence above their colleagues, apparently even enlisting their mother's help. And of course we know Thomas because he wanted more proof. One might almost say, "Better to be Thaddeus, about whom nothing is said, than to be Peter, James, John, or Thomas whom we remember especially because of their erratic ways."

Take it or leave it, these twelve are the transition between the old Israel (the blood descendants of Abraham, Isaac, and Jacob) and the new Israel (the spiritual descendants of Abraham, the new people of faith by way of Jesus the Christ). The end of the story, the New Jerusalem, the better Eden, is built symbolically on the twelve tribes of Israel and the twelve apostles (one of whom is eventually a substitute, Mathias). And consider a special irony if you will, that the son of Israel, Judah, through whom the messianic line descends, bears the same name as the failed disciple, Judas.

Jesus came "announcing God's good news," saying, "Now is the time! Here comes God's kingdom! Change your hearts and lives, and trust this good news!" (Mark 1:14-15). Wherever Jesus went, he called people to repentance so they would be ready for God's kingdom. Sometimes he said that the kingdom of God was coming, and sometimes that the kingdom of God was already there within them. He explained that God's kingdom was like a mustard seed: small to the point of inconsequence, yet eventually a tree in which birds can nest. And the kingdom is like a yeast, so small and yet when a woman hides it in a bushel of wheat flour the yeast works "its way through all the dough" (Matthew 13:33). And the kingdom is priceless. When someone discovers it, they're "full of joy," so excited that they sell "everything" in order to buy the field where the treasure is found (Matthew 13:44). Jesus trusted these very human disciples to begin ushering in the kingdom.

Jesus embodied the kingdom. He did so by embracing those who were otherwise seen as outsiders and therefore to be excluded. When John the Baptist sent his disciples for confirmation that Jesus was indeed the promised one, Jesus answered, "Go, report to John what you hear and see. Those who were blind are able to see. Those who were crippled are walking. People with skin diseases are cleansed. Those who were deaf now hear. Those who were dead are raised up. The poor have good news proclaimed to them" (Matthew 11:4-5). The ones Jesus identified as proof of his calling were the rejected ones, the people whose physical handicaps made them fit only to beg in that first-century world, or with leprosy, to be shut out of normal human relationships. As for the poor, they crowded in on Jesus. As the King James Version puts it, "the common people heard him gladly" (Mark 12:37). Jesus chose to eat with those whom society despised, such as the tax collectors—who were seen as collaborators with the Roman government—and prostitutes, as well as those who were exiled by severe and sometimes violent mental and emotional conditions, who were seen as demon-possessed. For such as these, Jesus was the kingdom come because he brought them in from their isolation and rejection and gave them worth that the culture of the times could not see.

Now Jesus expected his disciples to do the same. "He called his twelve disciples and gave them authority over unclean spirits to throw them out and to heal every disease and every sickness" (Matthew 10:1). In their first assignment they were to go only to the people of Israel; this was the beginning place. But it was only the beginning. When Jesus departed, by way of his ascension some weeks after the resurrection, he told them to be his "witnesses in Jerusalem, in all Judea and Samaria, and to the end of the earth" (Acts 1:8).

And somehow, they did it. These naturally provincial men, who had measured their world by the Sea of Galilee and its environs, moved out and out and out.

Without a doubt, the first disciples, the people we call "apostles," deserve a place in the biblical story—and thus in the unfolding history of God's purposes for this universe. Try as we will, it's hard to categorize them. They don't fit into the usual historical classifications the way kings, dictators, generals, and presidents do. Nor, for that matter, do they classify with popes (perhaps Peter, in the theology of the Catholic Church), bishops, or reformers. What name do you give to fishermen, tax collectors, and such who travel about the world of their time, talking as gladly with a slave as with a king, sure that each is of sublime importance with the God whom they represent, confident that each letter written, each speech given, each easy passing conversation, and each prayer is of eternal significance? What shall we say of such?

Perhaps they are the very embodiment of Jesus's parables. They are veritable mustard seeds, bits of leaven in the flour of the earth. Perhaps, just as some days Jesus looked at the lilies in the field and said that they were more glamorous than Solomon's regal garb, perhaps he also said, as he looked at Nathanael, Andrew, or James, "You're the salt of the earth! The world would be weary, dreary, and tasteless without you." We call them heroes now, but at times along the way—especially when they forsook Jesus—they looked more like rogues. Perhaps their primary classification is "the rest." Perhaps where some of us often are.

CHAPTER 10

Martha and Several Marys: They Also Serve Who Only Stand and Serve

Can we tell the history of our human race by way of biography without including key women? Until well into the twentieth century, secular history seemed content to do so. Yes, along the way were Cleopatra, Elizabeth I, and Victoria, to mention the obvious. In literature were the Brontë sisters, George Eliot, Emily Dickinson, and Louisa May Alcott. In science, Madame Marie Curie won two Nobel prizes in science, one in physics, and another in chemistry in a period of nine years. But for many centuries women seem overlooked in our history books.

Is it any different in the Bible's story of our human race? Some would answer, perhaps bitterly, not at all. Still, you certainly can't tell Adam's story without Eve, or do justice to Abraham's story without Sarah and Hagar. And to speak of Israel as a nation there must be mention of Miriam and Deborah, and Delilah and Abigail. And yes, Bathsheba. All of these women had major roles in the story—sometimes as leaders and sometimes as victims— but the story wouldn't have happened without them. Should the role of women have been more prominent? By my tastes, yes, and probably also by the standards of the twenty-first century in the Western world. But the biblical story was lived out in the culture of its times, for both good and ill, and an objective analysis suggests that we should probably be impressed by the comparative frequency with which women were factors in the Bible's unfolding plot.

As I read and reread the New Testament—particularly the four Gospels—I wonder if the authors were seeking in a subtle way to make a case for women in a world that was largely unsympathetic with such a message. As you know, there are two ways to make a point: direct confrontation and subtle persuasion. Subliminal advertising is the subtlest form of persuasion, the method by which an advocate plants ideas in our minds without our knowing it. Subtle persuasion is at its best in a setting where prejudice rides high. The person or persons speaking are sure no one can answer the accusations they're making against another individual or cause; then someone quietly offers a balancing word or an unsettling question. With such, discussion enters new territory.

The apostle Paul sometimes used confrontation. We're so accustomed to some of his words that we don't realize how thoroughly he was in the face of the opposition. In a world that was divided between slave and free, Jew and Gentile, women and men, Paul dared to say, "There is neither Jew nor Greek; there is neither slave nor free; nor is there male and female, for you are all one in Christ Jesus" (Galatians 3:28). He was announcing a new era—an era that still stumbles short of complete fulfillment in our time, even in the most enlightened areas of the world, and that would be heard with scorn and resentment in vast areas of our world in this twenty-first century.

But what of subtle persuasion? What of Matthew, Mark, Luke, and John—the premier biographers of Jesus?

For one, women are key at the beginning of the story. See how Matthew tells it. Having given us an obligatory genealogy, he comes to the story proper: "This is how the birth of Jesus Christ took place. When Mary his mother was engaged to Joseph, before they were married, she became pregnant by the Holy Spirit" (Matthew 1:18). The first character following the name of Jesus Christ is a woman, a teenage girl in fact. Luke—poet, storyteller, and historian that he was—begins with two women. First, there was Elizabeth. She enters the story by way of her husband, the priest Zechariah, but it is Elizabeth's credentials, strangely, that Luke emphasizes: "Elizabeth was a descendant of Aaron" (Luke 1:5). Aaron bungled some things badly in his time, but he was nevertheless Israel's first high priest and thus in a class by himself. Elizabeth can't be a high priest, of course, but in time she enjoys an assignment that makes her more memorable to the salvation story than generations of unnamed and forgotten high priests.

That is, she becomes in her old age the mother of a child known to us as John the Baptist. And she is the refuge and strength to her cousin, the village girl Mary. Because as soon as Mary learns that she is to have a baby by the Holy Spirit, she hurries for counsel not to her mother, but to Elizabeth. Elizabeth is then the first to acknowledge the infant in the womb for who he is: "With a loud voice [Elizabeth] blurted out, 'God has blessed you above all women, and he has blessed the child you carry. Why do I have this honor, that the mother of my Lord should come to me?'" (Luke 1:42-43). The birth of Jesus is very much a women's event, and it is a woman, Elizabeth, who recognizes its full significance.

Thirty-three years later, at Jesus's death and resurrection, women again are at the center of the story. Matthew tells us that on the night of Jesus's betrayal and arrest, "all the disciples left Jesus and ran away" (Matthew 26:56). It isn't ours to pass judgment on them because we weren't there, and it's essentially impossible to say what we would do in a situation we can't fairly imagine. And of course it's rarely if ever our business to pass judgment on another person. At that moment, the disciples knew that as the immediate companions of Jesus they were liable to the same fate. So they ran.

The next day, as Jesus was dying by crucifixion, the disciples were still not to be found. But Matthew gives us a detail that we tend to overlook. "Many women were watching from a distance. They had followed Jesus from Galilee to serve him. Among them were Mary Magdalene, Mary the mother of James and Joseph, and the mother of Zebedee's sons" (27:55-56).

Several things stand out in that short paragraph. There were "*many* women." This is not a precise figure, but it's clearly a sizeable number. Most of them remain anonymous, but whoever they were they had come from Galilee, following Jesus. This contradicts our picture of first-century women. Generally speaking, women were economically subservient, dependent almost entirely on the male world: beginning with a father, then a husband and/or brothers. Yet somehow these women were so committed to Jesus and his mission that they had broken free from the culture pattern of their time and had traveled to Jerusalem to support Jesus's work. Specifically, they were there to *serve* Jesus. They didn't have the distinction of being named apostles or of being called disciples; they were there to *serve*.

Serve isn't a premier word in our contemporary culture. But in the vocabulary of Jesus it is the calling above all others. "Whoever wants to be great among you will be your servant," Jesus told his disciples, and then reminded them (and us) that he "didn't come to be served but rather to serve" (Matthew 20:26, 28). We find this hard to believe even in the church. The women from Galilee understood it better than the twelve.

When Joseph of Arimathea took Jesus down from the cross and with Nicodemus's help carried the body to a place of burial, Mary Magdalene "and the other Mary" followed to the tomb, so they would know where Jesus was buried. Then, "at dawn" on the first day of the week—the day we now call Easter—these women came to the tomb. Their purpose, Luke tells us, was to bring spices for burial. They found the tomb empty, then ran to tell the disciples what they had found. Peter and John came and examined the tomb and returned home. But Mary Magdalene stayed, and was the first to see the resurrected Jesus. Just as it was women who were first to know of Jesus's birth, it was a company of women who stood at a distance during his death, two who followed to the place of burial, and one who was the first to witness the resurrection.

In the years between Jesus's conception and resurrection, women continued to have what some might call cameo appearances. I see them as more than that. As we noted earlier, when Joseph and Mary brought Jesus to the temple for the rites of purification—an event primarily for the mother—there were two aged saints to hail the occasion: Simeon and Anna, a prophet. Anna not only "began to praise God" after seeing Jesus, she also went on "to speak about Jesus to everyone who was looking forward to the redemption of Jerusalem" (Luke 2:38). That is, she was the first to declare a theology of salvation.

In stories that follow, women are often persons in need. In a sense there's nothing extraordinary about this because most of Jesus's encounters were with people in need. This is the essence of who Jesus was and is; he came to seek and to save the lost, whether male or female, young or old, helpless or exalted. We humans are all needy in one fashion or another. But Jesus's meetings with women often had a unique quality of human poverty.

I think, for instance, of the day Jesus interrupted a burial procession in the city of Nain. The deceased was a man. Luke puts it succinctly: "He was his mother's only son, and she was a widow" (Luke 7:12). She was both financially and emotionally destitute. Jesus "had compassion for her and said, 'Don't cry'" (7:13). Jesus then touched the stretcher and told the young man to "get up," and "Jesus gave him to his mother" (7:15). Obviously Jesus didn't stop every procession. Most of the time, Jesus gave his help to those who requested it—a request was in itself an expression of faith, however limited it might be. But in this instance Jesus interrupted in mercy without an invitation. He did it for a woman.

Once it was a woman who was quick on her intellectual feet. She was a Canaanite with a big problem, a daughter who was "suffering terribly from demon possession" (Matthew 15:22). Jesus seemed to ignore her pathetic appeal, and his disciples found her irritating. But when the woman overheard Jesus tell his disciples that his ministry was only to the people of Israel, she pressed her case. Now Jesus seemed to discourage her in language she would understand: "It is not good to take the children's bread and toss it to dogs" (15:26)—"dogs" being the common word a Jew might use for Gentiles. This clever woman took Jesus's metaphor and turned it to her advantage: "Yes, Lord, but even the dogs eat the crumbs that fall off their masters' table" (15:27). Jesus praised her faith and healed her child.

I wonder if Jesus had a woman like this in mind when he made a widow the delightful hero of one of his parables. The widow appealed to "a judge who neither feared God nor respected people" (Luke 18:2). The judge tried to ignore her, but the widow refused to be ignored. Jesus used the story to encourage prayer even when it seemed that the prayer was getting nowhere.

Speaking as I was a moment ago of a woman with a quick reply, no one was better at this kind of verbal riposte than a woman of Samaria. She was an outsider for sure, married five times and living now with a man to whom she was not married. Her story comes to us in the Gospel of John shortly after the story of the visit to Jesus by Nicodemus, one of the intellectual and spiritual leaders of his day; but in a sense, the anonymous woman of Samaria was more fluent in her discourse with Jesus than was Nicodemus. I suspect it was because the Samaritan woman had nothing to lose. Furthermore, she was used to defending herself because probably almost everyone was against her. Jesus chose to identify himself as the Messiah to this woman, a declaration that he otherwise held almost exclusively to his disciples. She receives extraordinary praise from John's

Gospel: "Many Samaritans in that city believed in Jesus because of the woman's word" (John 4:39).

If the Canaanite woman and the woman of Samaria are notable for parrying with Jesus, another woman won out by a combination of timidity and persistence. She had lived with a physical ailment which in her world was also a social disability. She had been bleeding for twelve years and, by the ancient law of Israel, any such bleeding classified a person as ritually unclean. Furthermore, anything such a person touched was unclean. Thus, for twelve years she had been a social outcast, cut off from friendship and normal affection. She believed Jesus could heal her but she felt she dare not reveal her condition.

So instead of asking for healing, she edged her way through the crowds so she could touch just the hem of Jesus's robe. She was healed immediately and Jesus sensed that power had gone out from him. When he asked who had touched him, the woman "came trembling" to identify herself. Jesus then did a continuing work of grace; he accepted her publicly and sent her away with the blessing of peace (Luke 8:43-48).

In several instances Jesus chose to challenge the religious establishment in his defense of a woman. He had done so, of course, when he touched the burial instrument for the son of the widow of Nain, because to touch such an instrument was to become unclean. One of the several times that Jesus confronted the religious leadership in their interpretation of Sabbath laws—perhaps the most crucial issue to the Jewish authorities, and with reason—was for the healing of a woman who "was bent over and couldn't stand up straight" (Luke 13:11). She had been in this condition for eighteen years. She didn't appeal to Jesus for healing; instead, he sought her out, placed his hands on her, and gave her immediate deliverance. This took place on the Sabbath. The religious leaders argued that Jesus could have waited for any other of the six days of the week instead of "working" on the Sabbath in this act of healing. Jesus replied with vigor, indeed, with anger, calling his accusers hypocrites. To make his point still more forceful he referred to the woman as "a daughter of Abraham"—that is, that she was as entitled to God's blessing as any man in the crowd since she, too, was descended spiritually and physically from their revered ancestor, Abraham.

Another instance came, according to the Gospel of John, when Mary, the sister of Martha and Lazarus, anointed Jesus's feet with expensive perfume, then dried his feet with her hair. Some objected because of the waste and no doubt all were offended at Mary's violation of "good taste." Jesus reasoned, however, that she had acted prophetically, preparing him for his burial.

Jesus's most dramatic defense of a woman in trouble is on an occasion when a group of "legal experts and Pharisees brought a woman caught in adultery" (John 8:3). Now of course it takes two to commit adultery and under the Jewish law both parties were equally culpable, but somehow the legal authorities hadn't managed to get the man. They were ready, however, to apply the whole power of the law on the woman. Jesus dismissed them with consummate ease, by turning their attention to their sins rather than to the sins of the woman. He made no attempt to deny the charges against the woman; he spoke one simple, profound sentence: "Whoever hasn't sinned should throw the first stone" (8:7). Those brief words have become one of the most familiar quotations in human thought. Probably a majority of people who quote it have no idea where it came from. It saved the woman's life, and it compelled her accusers to share her guilt. Jesus didn't approve of her sin—"Go, and from now on, don't sin anymore" (8:11). But in that very command he declared his belief in her ability to live a new life. His command was a vote of confidence.

These stories of Jesus's loving attention to women in need are beautiful. We can't tell them often enough, nor will we ever find the eloquence to do them justice. But their stories absorb us so much that we almost forget the part women played in the continuing biblical drama. As we have noted, there were women at the beginning of Jesus's story—Mary, Elizabeth, and Anna—and at the crucifixion and resurrection. But women were indispensable in Jesus's day-by-day ministry.

We get a tender picture of this in the home of Martha, Mary, and Lazarus, where Jesus was often a guest. One such occasion brought a confrontation between the sisters because Martha, "preoccupied with getting everything ready for their meal" (Luke 10:40), became frustrated with her sister who sat listening to Jesus. It's interesting, however, that we find the same scenario unfolding at a later time when we read again that "Martha served" the meal (John 12:2). Hospitality is a particular virtue. It is made up of many parts, some common and some aesthetic but all significant. The heart of hospitality is love. Not fashion, not returning a courtesy, not hope of advancement, but love. This kind of hospitality restored and strengthened Jesus as it still restores and strengthens all of us at repeated times of life. In the first-century home the man may have been the key figure, but the woman was the heart of hospitality.

It was women who provided economic support for Jesus's work. Luke reports that as Jesus "traveled through the cities and villages, preaching and proclaiming the good news of God's kingdom," the Twelve were traveling with him and also "some women who had been healed of evil spirits and sicknesses." We don't know how many, but Luke says that "among them" were Mary Magdalene, Joanna (who was the wife of Herod's servant Chuza), and Susanna, "and many others who provided for them out of their resources" (Luke 8:1-3). This was a culture where money traveled mainly through male hands, yet here were women who "provided" for Jesus and the disciples "out of their resources." Some of these same women, of course, were present at the crucifixion. They were among the most loyal of Jesus's followers, yet most of them are anonymous, and those whose names we know are largely without further identification.

The key word for these great souls is that they *served*. I repeat, it is not a sought-after role in our culture. It is a particularly unattractive word for this chapter on New Testament women in the biblical plotline; many women reading this chapter want at this point to say, "We've been servants long enough. It's time now to be executives."

Let me speak two words. For one, the best executives are those who know how to serve. The pompous and strutting are better for comic relief than for accomplishment.

But more than that, I'm making a case for the Christlike life. When the twelve disciples were arguing over "which one of them should be regarded as the greatest," Jesus explained an utterly new hierarchy of greatness: "The greatest among you must become like a person of lower status and the leader like a servant" (Luke 22:24, 26).

The kingdoms of this world—political, economic, social—so often are led by those who strut and then fall. The kingdom of God—the eternal kingdom—is led by servants. Among the earliest followers of Jesus, women showed us how to be kingdom people.

CHAPTER 11

Paul: The Peripatetic Theologian

It is impossible to tell the Bible by way of biographies without including the apostle Paul. Readers will have quite different opinions, however, as to the place we give to him, and sometimes very emphatic opinions. Some will argue that he merits more than one chapter since he was the premier convert, the ultimate missionary, and the founding theologian of the church. Others might concede that evaluation yet still resent the pages Paul receives, except as a place to argue with him as a person and as a theologian. Wherever you stand, however, you must confront Paul. You can't ignore him and tell the biblical story.

We know very little about Paul as a person. We know that he called Tarsus home; before we know him as Paul the Apostle we know him as Saul of Tarsus. At that time, Tarsus was the major city in Cilicia, in the province of Syria, and Paul was proud to identify his citizenship there. In addition to being an important commercial center, it was also a seat of learning; some would compare it in its time with Athens and Alexandria. This helps us understand Paul's love for learning and his ease in the company of scholars. It also makes one marvel all the more that he dedicated so much of his time and ministry to some of the poorest and least esteemed people.

His birth name, Saul, is significant. His heritage was in the tribe of Benjamin, and the most notable figure in that tribe's history was King Saul, the first king of Israel. We see Saul as a failed king—tragically so, as we indicated earlier. But descendants of the tribe of Benjamin didn't see him that way, and no doubt when Paul's parents named him Saul it was an expression of the dreams they entertained for their son's future. It must also have been a declaration of pride in their tribal heritage, a pride that Paul also felt.

Like many Jews in his day, Paul had two names, the Semitic name of his Jewish heritage and a Latin or Greek cognomen, which could be either a surname or a nickname. "Paulus" meant "little." Some feel that his family may have called him "Paulus" because of his diminutive appearance. As an adult, Paul apparently didn't cut a striking figure; thus Paul reminded the people of Corinth that they said of him, "His letters are weighty and strong, but his bodily presence is weak" (2 Corinthians 10:10). Whatever the connections between Paul's Latin name and his appearance, that name—Paul—became the name by which he was known as he ministered more and more in the Gentile world. Thus today we generally say "Saul of Tarsus" when we think of the unconverted man, and "Paul" as the apostle. In truth, one name is as truly his as the other.

On several occasions, in his letters and in speeches in the book of Acts, Paul tells us of his ancestry, his education, and his vigorous commitment to Judaism, yet he says nothing about his parents. We don't know their names, nor do we know his father's work. His father must have been a person of some standing since he was a Roman citizen—a citizenship that Paul inherited—yet we don't know what that work was. We learn later that Paul had a sister and a nephew, but we know of no other siblings or kin. And of course we don't know if he was ever married, though both scholars and casual readers speculate on the question and try variously to prove their conclusion.

When we first meet Paul he is a "young man" who is present at the trial of Stephen before the Jerusalem Council. But he is already a young-man-on-the-rise. Thus when a group of vehement leaders rise up to stone Stephen—an act they see as a service to God—they "laid their coats at the feet of a young man named Saul" (Acts 7:58 NRSV). The historian, Luke, reports this event a generation later, after Paul has become a key figure among the followers of Christ, but he is reflecting the esteem in which Saul was already held among the Jewish leaders. Luke concludes the story of Stephen's martyrdom by noting, "Saul approved of their killing him" (Acts 8:1 NRSV).

The book of Acts makes clear that the established Jewish religious leadership, assisted by the Roman government, set out to destroy the fledgling Christian movement. Apparently Saul became one of the most vocal and physical in this effort. "Saul was still spewing out murderous threats against the Lord's disciples" (Acts 9:1). He got authority from the high priest to seek out such persons in Damascus, "whether men or women," and it was while Paul was on this mission that his life was turned altogether around. The man who intended to become the chief opponent of the followers of Christ became instead their most effective spokesperson (9:2).

Nearly every other conversion story in the New Testament is told in a sentence or two: essentially it is, "Jesus said, 'Follow me,' and they rose up and followed him." But with Paul we get a longer story. Mind you, it is still brief (though novelists, poets, dramatists, and preachers have been expanding on it ever since), but we're given the full dialogue. The book of Acts reports it not just once, but three times: in the account of the event itself (9:1-9), in Paul's testimony before an unruly crowd in Jerusalem (22:6-16), and in Paul's testimony before King Agrippa (26:12-17).

To say that this was the turning point in Saul's life is to state the obvious. Every conversion is a turning around: where once we were living for self we now live for Christ. Probably only a few of us, however, have such a spectacular turning-around as Saul did. Yet every conversion is a miracle because, if the course of one's life is reversed, the change is eternal in its fruit and its consequences. The degree of drama depends partly on the intensity with which one was previously going in the opposite direction. Saul is not the last to experience such a dramatic turning-around; such spiritual biographies are still being written daily in every part of the world. But Saul's story leads the way. And not only because of the fervor with which he previously opposed Christ, but because of the results that followed his conversion.

What are the results? How is it that we single out Paul as a biographical character on whom the biblical story partially rests—and thus also the human story to which the Bible speaks?

We're struck first by Paul's complete reversal. There's nothing tentative about it. He was heading to Damascus at full speed, intent on arresting and prosecuting some converts there when "suddenly a light from heaven encircled him," he fell to the ground and heard a voice asking why he was persecuting him. The people traveling with Saul picked him up and took him to the city. He was blind for three days. He then met with a Christian believer, Ananias, who counseled him in his new faith and prayed for him. Saul regained his sight, was baptized, and ate after three days without food or water. Luke tells us that Saul stayed with the disciples in Damascus for several days and that "Right away, he began to preach about Jesus in the synagogues. 'He is God's Son,' he declared" (Acts 9:20). So it is that he began within days to declare the faith that a few days earlier he had sought to destroy—and with the same intensity. And from the outset it is a theological statement. But notice a dramatic difference. When he was seeking to destroy the faith he had the backing of the leadership of his people, the Jews, and with it the tacit support of the Roman government. Now he was allying himself with a rag-tag group of believers—few if any outstanding people among them—who were very small in number and unfavorably notorious. It took some deep conviction to make such a change—a change that would shape and direct his life until his martyrdom.

Then came a sorry surprise. The very people to whom Paul had committed himself, the followers of Christ, doubted him. Perhaps it isn't surprising. Persecution had made them a close-knit group and it had to be difficult for any newcomer fully to break in—especially a newcomer who had once arrested and prosecuted their very friends and fellow believers, and who was so different from them. Most of the original disciples were common folk, Galileans, while Paul was an intellectual, a man of the world, and a social sophisticate.

Eventually, with the help of Barnabas, one of the greatest of the saints, Paul began to come into his full calling. It's difficult to define it. Some call him the first Christian missionary. There's irony in this because when Jesus gave the great command, "go therefore and make disciples of all nations" (Matthew 28:19), Paul wasn't there to receive the call and its authority, since this was several years before his conversion. Yet, when we look at the maps in the back of a Bible, it is Paul's missionary journeys that are charted for us, not those of any original disciple. Indeed, when the Lord called Ananias to meet with Saul of Tarsus, Paul is described as "the agent I have chosen to carry my name before Gentiles, kings, and Israelites" (Acts 9:15). Paul seemed to understand from the beginning that he was an apostle to the Gentiles (Romans 11:13). And when he was inclined to stay in Asia Minor, he received a vision that compelled him to go over into what we now call Europe to carry the message where others had not yet gone. Paul came to glory in the fact that he went into new territories rather than building on the work of predecessors. So yes, Paul was the quintessential missionary. Tradition says that nearly all, if not all, of the apostles (including Matthias, the successor to Judas) went far from their original Galilean settings, but nobody did so with such breadth of territory and such passion for moving on as did Paul.

But if Paul was the first great missionary and church planter, he was just as surely the basic icon of the pastor. In a very real sense, this is what the letters of Paul are all about. They are theological and ethical documents, no doubt about that, but their basic business is pastoral. Paul was a lifelong pastor, not a short-term leader. He preached in a place sometimes for weeks and sometimes for a year or more, and he never allowed those churches to leave his heart or his supervision. He waited for word regarding their welfare, and when he got information he wrote pastoral documents in response. He saw the people in these churches not only as his brothers and sisters in Christ but also in many instances as his children in the faith. He described himself as being jealous for their welfare. And yes, sometimes we sense that he was also jealous of their loyalty to him. If ever a person was a pastor through and through, it was Paul. Thus the letters to Timothy and Titus are classified as pastoral letters because in them we have instruction to young leaders in the church as to how they should go about their calling. Paul wanted to be sure that the leaders who followed him took care of the souls he left behind. Scholarship divides as to whether Paul wrote the letters to Timothy and Titus or whether they were written by Paul or by someone who was speaking in Paul's name and presumed authority. The point remains the same, however: in the early church, Paul was the pastoral icon. His letter to Philemon is a classic pastoral document, as he seeks on one hand to protect the welfare of the runaway slave Onesimus who is now one of Paul's converts, while at the same time counseling Onesimus's owner, Philemon, in his Christian responsibility.

Paul saw himself as an apostle. Obviously, he didn't belong to the original twelve. And of course he never saw Jesus in the flesh. Nevertheless, if anyone deserved to be called an apostle, it was certainly Paul. It's interesting that he cherished this recognition so much. When we see him listing his achievements, the suffering he endured for the sake of the gospel, and the energy with which he labored (all of it by comparison with others), it's clear that Paul always saw himself as something of an outsider among the original followers of Jesus. Surely there's something ironic about this, and we can probably learn from it.

However, with all of Paul's accomplishments as a missionary, an evangelist, and a pastor, his singular role for the ages is that of Christianity's original theologian—the theologian to whom all future generations pay obeisance—some by quoting him with their support and others by seeking to discredit or disprove him.

Many in this generation—and in previous ones, too—resent Paul for his role as a theologian, simply because they dislike the idea of theology being "imposed" on their understanding of Jesus. This kind of thinking sees Jesus as an uncomplicated, admirable figure, one who accepted people as they were and who readily forgave them their shortcomings. They see him as especially attentive to children, to the poor, to women in general, to widows in particular, and to even the most disreputable of sinners.

This description of Jesus is altogether true. Indeed, put it in bold type because this description also gives us a clearer picture of God. Thus when the disciple Philip asked, "Lord, show us the Father; that will be enough for us," Jesus answered, "Whoever has seen me has seen the Father" (John 14:8-9). As soon as we read such a statement from Jesus, we realize not only that Jesus gives us a fuller understanding of God but that he also is compelling us to do some theologizing. After all, who is this Jesus that he made such claims for himself?

So Paul set out to teach new believers. It was a formidable task. The earliest of them were Jews, who had a knowledge of the Hebrew Scriptures and with it an expectation of the Messiah, the Christ. It's likely, however, that before Paul's martyrdom a majority of believers were Gentiles, people who had no prior knowledge of God, other than the innate human longing for a

God who would fit the description that Jesus embodied in both his person and his teaching.

Paul filled in the details in humanity's rough sketch of longing, and he did so with a breathtaking flourish. He explained that Jesus "was in the form of God," but that "he emptied himself,... becoming like human beings," even

> becoming obedient to the point of death,
> even death on a cross.
> Therefore, God highly honored him
> and gave him a name above all names,
> so that at the name of Jesus everyone
> in heaven, on earth, and under the earth might bow
> and every tongue confess that
> Jesus Christ is Lord, to the glory of God the Father.
> (Philippians 2:6-11)

Paul also tells us that Jesus Christ

> is the image of the invisible God,
> the one who is first over all creation,
> Because all things were created by him:
> both in the heavens and on the earth, [including]
> the things that are visible and the things that are invisible.

This is because "He existed before all things, / and all things are held together in him." Of course, "Because all the fullness of God / was pleased to live in him" (Colossians 1:15-17, 19).

It is Paul who gives us our understanding of the cross—"a scandal to the Jews and foolishness to the Gentiles," but for those who accept it, "God's power and God's wisdom," and "the power of God for those of us who are being saved" (1 Corinthians 1:23-24, 18). We take it for granted that the cross is central to the faith (perhaps to the discomfort of some), a symbol over not only churches, but hospitals, schools, various ministries of mercy, and cemeteries, but it was Paul who first dared insist that this despised instrument of torture and execution was at the very heart of the faith. "God forbid," he wrote to believers in Galatia who were confused in their theology, "God forbid that I should boast about anything except for the cross of our Lord Jesus Christ" (Galatians 6:14).

It was Paul, too, who joined history and theology for the resurrection event. The four Gospels each conclude with resurrection stories, but in First Corinthians Paul gives a summary of some of the events and then explains the significance of it all and answers some of the very simple but perplexing questions people were asking. He begins his report, "Christ died for our sins in line with the scriptures, he was buried, and he rose on the third day in line with the scriptures" (1 Corinthians 15:3-4). Like all of the New Testament writers, Paul relates the events in Jesus's life with the Hebrew Scriptures, and of course Paul had a wealth of learning on which to draw. Paul weaves together the Easter story and its meaning for believers in the promise of the resurrection of our mortal bodies. Again, theology—theology applied to the fears and questions of the people. This again is Paul the pastor and theologian. His teaching is always related to the life and concern of the believer, never simply detached information.

Paul also gives us our theology of the church, the "body of Christ." He understands the struggles believers have in their daily pilgrimage, reminds them that "we win a sweeping victory through the one who loved us," because "nothing can separate us from God's love in Christ Jesus" (Romans 8:37-38). He reassures us in our prayer life: when we don't know how to pray "the Spirit itself pleads our case with unexpressed groans" (8:26). He lifts our spirits with the assurance that "God works all things together for good for the ones who love God" (8:28). And along the way he opens his heart to us, letting us know of his own struggles and confiding that in a matter where he needed so much to get an affirmative answer to his prayer, God told him instead that he would be provided with grace enough to carry on with a negative answer (2 Corinthians 12:8).

And he did it all with letters. Mind you, he taught in person in the first century, but fortunately—providentially!—he put a great deal in writing, and the churches and persons that got the letters saved them and made copies, laboriously, with primitive materials, passing them on from church to church. And we have them today. Thus Paul's theology is a theology of life—life in the marketplace, the bedroom, the courtroom, and the church supper, the loneliness of death, the disagreements in church meetings, the struggles of prayer, and the grandeur of transformed lives. The data may sometimes be difficult to understand, but it never lacks passion. And profound as it is, it is never theoretical. It is as practical as the man who shaped some of its structure in his mind while he was sewing on a leather tent or pacing the floor of imprisonment. It is faith to be lived with because Paul lived it before and lived it while he spoke it. It is impossible to imagine the biblical story without the man from Tarsus, blinded by God's light so that in time he saw better than anyone, then passed his vision on to us.

CHAPTER 12

Jesus Christ: The Son of God and the Son of Humanity

A s surely as this book had to begin with God, it must conclude with Jesus the Christ. To put it in the language of
classical theology, the book begins and ends with God; at first,
as God is revealed in the Hebrew Scriptures (the Old Testament)
and then as revealed in the Christian extension of the Hebrew
Scriptures, the New Testament. Basic Christian theology would
also say that the Lord Christ was in the story from the beginning. More about that later!

How do we begin the story of Jesus, our Lord? Let me
do so with several paragraphs that will be familiar to some,

since these paragraphs sometimes appear on greeting cards or in various anthologies. Although often identified as "anonymous," the author was almost surely James Allan Francis, a native of Canada and a Baptist minister who included the lines in approximately this form in an address at a Baptist Young People's Union convention in Los Angeles in 1926:

> He was born in an obscure village, the child of a peasant woman. Until He was thirty, He worked in a carpenter shop and then for three years He was an itinerant preacher. He wrote no books. He held no office. He never owned a home. He was never in a big city.
>
> He never traveled two hundred miles from the place He was born. He never did any of the things that usually accompany greatness. The authorities condemned His teachings. His friends deserted Him. One betrayed Him to His enemies for a paltry sum. One denied Him. He went through the mockery of a trial.
>
> He was nailed on a cross between two thieves. While He was dying, His executioners gambled for the only piece of property He owned on earth: His coat. When He was dead He was taken down and placed in a borrowed grave.
>
> Nineteen centuries have come and gone, yet today he is the crowning glory of the

human race, the adored leader of hundreds
of millions of the earth's inhabitants.

All the armies that ever marched and all the
navies that were ever assembled and all the
parliaments that ever sat and all the rulers
that ever reigned—combined—have not
affected the life of man upon the earth so
profoundly as that One Solitary Life.

Dr. Francis took the raw outline of Jesus's life on this planet
and turned it into simple yet eloquent poetry. It's not surprising that Christmas cards, anthologies, and sermon writers have
quoted the author until his name is forgotten. This outline of
Jesus's life—all of it taken from the biblical story, which after all
is the only ancient document to give us the story—reminds us
that in many respects Jesus of Nazareth lived a life that is obviously memorable yet utterly commonplace.

That is, except for the miracles and for quotations from his
teachings, Jesus's story is a kind of symbolic picture of human
futility, the essence of being forgettable. He was born in obscurity and died the way literally thousands of people died in the
first-century world, by public execution, which was the Roman
government's formula for maintaining order. In between, like
most people, he had his moments. But in total, he had a bare
three years in public life, nearly all of it spent in a physical area
the size of a healthy county in America. We know of only two relatively significant persons who were drawn to him, Nicodemus
and Joseph of Arimathea, but they would be long forgotten if it
weren't for their interest in Jesus. The rest of Jesus's followers
were the most common of the common—"people of the earth"
was their usual classification. Jesus seemed to go out of his way

to associate with those who would bring discredit to him: prostitutes and publicans. Yet today he is the standard of measure for all others. Thus students of Abraham Lincoln will note that more books have been written about Lincoln than anyone other than Jesus.

How can this be for a person "born in obscurity," living out his earthly life in a region of the first-century world that was almost incidental to the glory of the Roman Empire? Come to think of it, when we refer to the times as "the first-century world," we pay unconscious tribute to Jesus because our calendar in the Western world—now operative in all the world—gets its identity in the birth of Jesus. We measure time by B.C. (before Christ) and A.D. (anno Domini, the year of our Lord). How can this be? In the language of the late Paul Harvey, where is "the rest of the story"?

As to specific data, Jesus was born in a town called Bethlehem. It was revered as the town from which Israel's greatest king, David, had come centuries before, but by Jesus's time it was simply another village. Two of the biblical biographers, Matthew and Luke, tell us of miracles attending his birth: that his conception was by the Holy Spirit and that the place of his birth was providentially Bethlehem because the prophet Micah had said it would be so (Micah 5:2). Luke also tells us that angels announced his birth, but to an unpretentious audience: shepherds on a hillside outside Bethlehem. Luke also tells us that when the baby was presented in the temple for the rite of purification, two saintly, elderly people, Anna and Simeon, hailed his birth as the fulfillment of prophecy; and Matthew reports that wise men came from the east in search of him because in their research they learned that he was to be the King of the Jews.

For a period of time the family went to Egypt to avoid the maniacal pursuit of King Herod, and then settled in the hill town of Nazareth, where Jesus lived in obscurity until he was thirty, except for a few days in his twelfth year that Luke records for us. At thirty he began to teach, to preach, and to heal. Growing numbers of people followed him, some drawn by his teaching and some by his miracles. He selected twelve from among these followers, to be his disciples—that is, students he would mentor. They were honorable men, but to an outsider they would appear to be quite ordinary, and thus easily forgotten.

Slowly, however, Jesus became a polarizing figure. In a sense, it's hard to see why. Mind you, if he had stuck to his teaching— "The kingdom of heaven is at hand"—the Roman government might have become disturbed. But the fact that his teaching was accompanied by healing couldn't help but take some of the political significance from what he was saying because it made him more of a kindly, personal figure rather than a voice of political reform. Besides, the kingdom talk itself was so unpolitical. There were no attacks on the Roman government as such. To the contrary, when Jesus said, "When they force you to go one mile, go with them two" (Matthew 5:41), he could have been seen as catering to the empire, since one of the most offensive practices of the occupying Roman soldiers was their right to commandeer any person to carry their military equipment for a mile. And surely any government official would smile at Jesus's political talk when he announced that his kingdom was like a grain of mustard seed, or a woman's stock of leaven, or a treasure hidden in a field. Only a quite neurotic official would see some conspiracy code in such teaching. Worse still for Jesus's political cause was the fact that the only leadership he attacked were the scribes and Pharisees ("hypocrites," he called them), who were religious leaders among the Jews, not political figures. The Romans were quick to put down any organized rebellion but it's hard to imagine that they would feel threatened by this wandering teacher who was known more for his healing, miracles, and attacks on the Jewish religious leaders than for any political acumen.

Nevertheless, something was afoot. The apostle Paul said that Jesus came in "the fullness of time" (Galatians 4:4, Ephesians 1:10 NRSV). To put it colloquially, the time was ripe. As a student of the Hebrew Scriptures, Paul could sense that the vision of the prophets and the dreams of the poets were now at the point of fulfillment; that is, that in the purposes of God, the world was ready for God's Messiah. When we see the frequency with which the New Testament writers quoted the Hebrew Scriptures in their attempts to grasp the wonder of Jesus the Christ we sense that there must have been among the devout untold conversations in the generations shortly before Jesus's birth about the one who was to come. It was not only that the devout came to see Jesus in the Hebrew Scriptures after his appearing, but that the pictures became more sharply defined as they prayed for the Messiah's coming.

The story of the wise men who came from the east in search of "the newborn king of the Jews" (Matthew 2:1-12) suggests that Gentiles, too, were waiting for a special person to come. Cold logic makes one ask why magi would bother themselves about a king of the Jews. At that point in the history of nations, the Jews could hardly have been called a nation. They had been without a homeland of their own for roughly six centuries, and even at its height Israel was marginal in the political and military affairs of the ancient world. Why would wise men—the military, political, and philosophical voices of their day—be interested in the possibility of a king born to what was essentially a nation without a homeland?

There is always a spiritual hunger in our world, but it is more pronounced in some periods than in others. At times the hunger seems almost to disappear and then again come periods of renewal. In the several generations prior to and surrounding Jesus's birth, this hunger seemed strangely widespread, and often among persons of respected insight. The late William Barclay noted that "just about the time when Jesus was born, there was in the world a strange feeling of expectation, a waiting for the coming of a king." Barclay cites historians of the general period, Suetonius in his *Life of Vespasian*, and Tacitus in his *Histories*, and a poet, too—the Roman, Virgil, who wrote in his Fourth Eclogue about golden days to come. "It was to a waiting world that Jesus came," Barclay concludes.[1] Is this the sort of thing the apostle Paul had in mind when he said that "the fullness of time" had come?

Christian hymns have memorialized this theme of ancient human longing. An anonymous poet of the ninth century gave voice to what he thought Israel must have felt:

> O Come, Emmanuel,
> and ransom captive Israel,
> that mourns in lonely exile here
> until the Son of God appear.

Midway through the eighteenth century, Charles Wesley spoke the same theme, and saw it as a universal hunger:

> Come, thou long-expected Jesus,
> born to set thy people free;

from our fears and sins release us,
let us find our rest in thee.
Israel's strength and consolation,
hope of all the earth thou art;
dear desire of every nation,
joy of every longing heart.[2]

However one looks at it, the story of Jesus has a majesty and a mystery all its own. Secular students of world religions seek out parallels in other ancient religious stories, but those stories are now known only to scholars who work with ancient and essentially forgotten documents; meanwhile the story of Jesus has gone to every part of the world. Indeed, in several hundred instances the reason people all around the world have a written language is because the followers of Christ labored to give written language to oral cultures so they might then give them the Christian Scriptures. Religious organizations are not always praised for their business acumen and efficiency and sometimes their internal squabbling has weakened their cause, yet somehow the message of Christ has gone to places otherwise thought inaccessible. In every century since Stephen, the first martyr, Christians have died by the hundreds, the thousands, and sometimes the tens of thousands for their faith, yet the faith has lived on and has grown.

How does one explain this? Most of us know the basic story, as we referred to it a few moments ago. A child was born to a teenage village girl, Mary; she was engaged to a carpenter, Joseph, but the baby born to her was understood to have been conceived by the Spirit of God. For thirty years he lived a life so uneventful that we have only one anecdote from all of those years. Then he set out to teach, and people gathered to him.

This was not remarkable, however; such teachers arose for a time, had their following, and were essentially forgotten within a decade or two of their lifetime.

To complicate the story further, Jesus died in ignominy by public execution. He was one among thousands who died in this fashion, crucifixion, in that period of Roman history. There was therefore every reason that he would be forgotten. Instead, the nature of his death has become the most familiar symbol on the skylines of villages and cities in nearly every part of the world, and is probably the world's most common item of jewelry—the cross.

However, something quite spectacular happened on the third day of his death, when he was raised from the dead. He was seen by numbers of his followers—over five hundred in one instance, according to the apostle Paul—over a period of forty days, after which he "ascended into heaven," as the Apostles' Creed puts it. Then, at exceeding personal peril the handful of his devoted followers began to tell the story. On the whole these first witnesses were not an impressive lot. Only one of them, Paul, could be called a scholar, though several proved to be eloquent writers, leaving behind documents that were copied by hand, distributed and preserved in numbers that eclipse what is left of the writings of Julius Caesar and a variety of admirable historians, poets, and dramatists of the same general period. How exactly could this happen?

Jesus of Nazareth is an appealing figure, no doubt about that. But appealing figures appear in every generation, adored by some and perhaps by many, but largely forgotten when their own generation is past. How is it that Jesus Christ continues to gain such a following? In Asia and Africa the numbers of believers is growing incrementally. Some 2.18 billion people in the world call themselves Christians—roughly one-third of the world population. Untold millions from that larger number are passionately devout, doing everything in their power to live as they think Jesus would have them live. Perhaps these are the leaven in the earth's lump to which Jesus referred, the salt of the earth that saves our human race from death by its own corruption.

Who then is he, this Jesus born in Bethlehem and now revered over the entire planet? One of his first biographers, John, said that he was the Word who was with God and who was God, from the very beginning (John 1:1-2). Paul said that he was "in the form of God," having equality with God, but that he chose to lay aside this power in order to become "like human beings" so that he might die on a cross, and that God has given him

> a name above all names,
>   so that at the name of Jesus everyone
>   in heaven, on earth, and under the
> earth might bow
> and every tongue confess that
> Jesus Christ is Lord, to the glory of God the Father.
>   (Philippians 2:6-11)

So it is that every week, every day, untold numbers of people receive the sacrament and say, "Christ has died, Christ has risen, Christ will come again."

I take John's word for it, and Paul's, and the classic theologians of the centuries, and indeed the witness of my own heart and that of thousands of believers I have known. Jesus was more than a winsome village teacher, more than a miracle worker, more than a premier teacher. He was, as the creed puts it, "very God of very God." Theodore Wedel, a leading Episcopal teacher and preacher in the mid-twentieth century, noted that Americans like success stories, on the "log cabin to White House" pattern, but that Jesus was the opposite of that story. For him, it was "White House to log cabin": he was the Son of God, of the very substance of God, but he became man at Bethlehem to save our human race.

It is for this that Jesus's "one solitary life" stands out. Not as a miracle worker, master teacher, or moral example, but as the Savior of humankind. This is what puts Jesus beyond comparisons: historic, yes, but eternal; to be admired, true, but far more, to be worshiped.

The biblical story of our planet and our human race begins in an Eden of perfection where God was very present. It concludes, in the book of Revelation, in a city of breathtaking beauty, where there is no longer any curse (Revelation 22:3), and the Lord God is ever present. It is better than Eden because good has triumphed.

It's quite a trip, marked all along the way with heroes aplenty and rogues, too. And mostly, "the rest." I suspect that you and I would probably classify ourselves among "the rest." But if I read the story rightly, God wills that we would all step up to the heroic level. To become, that is, persons whose lives are such that God's will is done on our particular piece of earth, even as it is in heaven.

Notes

1. In the Beginning, God

1. Francis Thompson, *The Hound of Heaven* (New York: Dodd, Mead, 1922), lines 3–4.

2. Adam and Eve

1. John Donne, *Devotions Upon Emergent Occasions,* 1624, Meditation XVII.

2. Frederick Buechner, *Godric* (New York: HarperCollins, 1983), 142.

3. Robert Alter, *The Five Books of Moses* (New York: W. W. Norton, 2004), 24.

4. Fleming Rutledge, *And God Spoke to Abraham* (Grand Rapids: Eerdmans, 2011), 62.

3. Abraham and Sarah

1. Kilian McDonnell, *Swift, Lord, You Are Not* (Collegeville, Minn.: Saint John's University Press, 2003), 10–11.

2. Rutledge, *And God Spoke to Abraham* 55.

3. I am interpreting this story on the basis of spiritual salvation, not in matters of natural disasters. In natural disasters some godly persons testify that God preserved them intact or with little loss, while other equally godly persons give thanks that their faith sustained them in the midst of physical and economic loss and even of bereavement.

4. Rutledge, *And God Spoke to Abraham,* 55.

4. Jacob and His Kin
1. Quoted from Francis Meynell, *Week-End Book: A Sociable Anthology* (London: Nonesuch Press, 1924).

5. Moses
1. Bruce Feiler, *America's Prophet: Moses and the American Story* (New York: HarperCollins, 2009), 67.
2. Feiler, *America's Prophet*, 283.

6. Samuel
1. Jerome Charyn, "Meditations on the First Book of Samuel and King Saul," in *Congregation: Contemporary Writers Read the Jewish Bible*, ed. David Rosenberg (New York: Harcourt Brace Jovanovich, 1987), 98.
Charyn, "Meditations," 99.

7. David
1. J. Ellsworth Kalas, *The Grand Sweep* (Nashville: Abingdon Press, 1996).
2. C. S. Lewis, *Reflections on the Psalms* (London: Geoffrey Bles, 1958), 2.
3. Mary Ellen Chase, *The Psalms for the Common Reader* (New York: W. W. Norton, 1962), 31.
4. John Paterson, *The Book That Is Alive* (New York: Charles Scribner's Sons, 1954), 58.
5. Paterson, *Book That Is Alive*, 59.
6. Charyn, "Meditations" 101.
7. Charyn, "Meditations," 102.

8. Elijah
1. John Paterson, *The Goodly Fellowship of the Prophets* (New York: Charles Scribner's Sons, 1948), 1–2.

9. Peter, James, and John
1. Justin Martyr, *Apologia*, I:39.

2. A. C. Bouquet, *Everyday Life in New Testament Times* (New York: Charles Scribner's Sons, 1954), 156–57.

12. Jesus Christ

1. William Barclay, *The Gospel of Matthew, Volume 1* (Philadelphia: Westminster, 1958), 18.

2. *The United Methodist Hymnal* (Nashville: The United Methodist Publishing House, 1989), 196.

Discussion Guide for
Heroes, Rogues, and the Rest
by J. Ellsworth Kalas

John D. Schroeder

CHAPTER 1
IN THE BEGINNING, GOD

Snapshot Summary

This chapter examines what we know about God, beginning with creation, God's plans, and God's relationship with us.

Reflection / Discussion Questions

1. What do you hope to gain by reading this book?
2. What is your perception of God? How has it changed over the years?
3. How do the biblical writers portray God?
4. List some of the names given to God in the Bible.
5. What do the biblical writers say about the origin of God? Why?
6. God is powerful. Give examples of God's power.
7. Describe the way God creates.
8. Give some examples showing the gracious nature of God.

9. How do we know God has a plan?
10. What is the most telling detail in the biography of God?

Prayer

Dear God, thank you for creating a wonderful world and for giving us the ability to have a relationship with you. Amen.

CHAPTER 2
ADAM AND EVE: OUR KIND OF PEOPLE

Snapshot Summary

This chapter continues the creation story with God creating Adam and Eve. It reminds us that God gives us choices, but with choices there are consequences.

Reflection / Discussion Questions

1. When you were young or in Sunday school, what did you learn about Adam and Eve?
2. What is the theological statement made in Genesis 1?
3. We humans are made in God's image: What does this mean?
4. How does Genesis 2 help us learn about God? What does it tell us?
5. Give your reaction to the statement: the breath that is in us is the very breath of God.
6. Humans are choice-makers. Give some consequences of our choices. How do we make choices?
7. Why and how did God create a female companion for Adam?

8. Give your view and evidence of the complexity of humans based on information from Genesis.
9. Why do you think Adam and Eve ate what was forbidden?
10. What does the story of Adam and Eve tell us about consequences?

Prayer

Dear God, thank you for giving us life, for giving us choices, and for always giving us your love. Amen.

CHAPTER 3
ABRAHAM AND SARAH: PIONEERS OF PROMISE

Snapshot Summary

This chapter begins with a look at the lives of Abraham and Sarah, including their faith and struggles.

Reflection / Discussion Questions

1. Why is Lamech notable? What is known about him?
2. What impresses you about Enoch and his story?
3. If you were to write a biography of Noah, what would you say about him?
4. How are Abraham and Sarah shapers of the biblical plot and story?
5. How does the story of Abraham begin?
6. What do you admire about the faith of Abraham? What lessons can be learned from his faith and life?

7. What does the Bible tell us about Sarah? How was she a hero?

8. Describe some of the struggles faced by Abraham, Sarah, and Hagar.

9. This chapter illustrates how God has faith in all of us. What does this mean to you?

10. What impresses you most in the story of Abraham and Sarah?

Prayer

Dear God, thank you for the faith and deeds of Abraham and Sarah and for having faith in us. Amen.

CHAPTER 4
JACOB AND HIS KIN: THE USES OF DYSFUNCTION

Snapshot Summary

This chapter tells the story of Jacob and his relatives, a dysfunctional family that teaches us about ourselves and God.

Reflection / Discussion Questions

1. Why is it important that the Bible is honest?

2. What type of person was Jacob? Name some of his faults and assets.

3. How did Jacob treat his brother? How was he treated by Laban?

4. Give some examples of the dysfunctional nature of Jacob's family.

5. What do you admire about Jacob's son Joseph?
6. Why do you think the story of Jacob is included in the Bible? Why is it important?
7. What does the life and story of Jacob tell us about God?
8. Do you think all families are dysfunctional to some degree? Explain.
9. What do you think is the oddest event in the story of Jacob and his family?
10. What lessons can we learn from the life of Jacob?

Prayer

Dear God, thank you for using us for your purposes, even with our dysfunctional nature and lack of faith. Amen.

CHAPTER 5
MOSES: FREEDOM TO OBEY

Snapshot Summary

This chapter examines the life and times of Moses. It shows us how God used Moses as a leader to help his people.

Reflection / Discussion Questions

1. What impresses you most as we continue this biographical journey?
2. Why do you think the people of Israel maintained a sense of significant identity during slavery?
3. Name some famous people throughout history who have been or who might be compared to Moses.
4. Explain why Moses's story is in a class by itself. Why is it so unique?

5. What is known about the birth and early years of Moses?
6. How and why did Moses go from adopted son of privilege to international fugitive?
7. When God gave Moses an assignment, how did Moses react? How did the Israelites react to the help of Moses?
8. Name some of the highs and lows that happened while Moses was Israel's leader.
9. What two pictures stand out in Moses's gallery? Describe him.
10. What lessons can we learn from the life of Moses?

Prayer

Dear God, thank you for providing us with leaders in times when we need faith and direction. Amen.

CHAPTER 6
SAMUEL: THE PURPOSES OF GOVERNMENT

Snapshot Summary

This chapter introduces us to the life and times of Samuel, a great soul who served God, and it also looks at the leaders and government that followed him.

Reflection / Discussion Questions

1. What situations and events were happening in Israel in this time period?
2. How was Eli positioned in life to help Samuel?
3. Why was Samuel effective early in his life as a spiritual and political leader?

4. How were the sons of Samuel like the sons of Eli? Why didn't Samuel see this?
5. Why did Israel want "a king...like all the other nations have"?
6. Explain why Samuel was a great soul.
7. What was Israel's reaction to the introduction of Saul as king?
8. Why did Saul not work out well as a king? What were his flaws?
9. Compare David to the previous leaders of Israel.
10. What do you admire about Samuel?

Prayer

Dear God, we thank you for guiding us through the good and bad times. Amen.

CHAPTER 7
DAVID: THE IMPORTANCE OF SINGING WHAT YOU THINK

Snapshot Summary

This chapter provides an overview of the wisdom books of the Bible—their poetry, songs, and praise to God.

Reflection / Discussion Questions

1. How do Psalms and Proverbs fit into the biblical story?
2. What is the connection of David and Solomon to the books of wisdom in the Bible?
3. How is Hebrew poetry in the Bible unlike other poetry?

4. Name and describe three forms of biblical poetry.
5. Describe the merits and purpose of the Psalms.
6. What is the place and importance of the book of Proverbs?
7. How do song lyrics enhance the Bible?
8. What is the connection between the wisdom of poetry and effective leadership?
9. How can the books of wisdom help us today? Why are they timeless?
10. Give your own summary of the importance of singing what you think.

Prayer

Dear God, thank you for the wisdom, songs, and poetry contained in the Bible. Help us treasure and use them. Amen.

CHAPTER 8
ELIJAH: VOICES IN THE WILDERNESS

Snapshot Summary

This chapter looks at the importance and contributions of prophets in the Bible, beginning with Elijah.

Reflection / Discussion Questions

1. How have "voices" played an important role throughout history?
2. What is meant by "voices in the wilderness"?
3. What role did the voices of the prophets play?
4. How was Elijah the embodiment of the prophetic tradition?

5. Give your thoughts on how Elijah was different from other prophets. In what way was he unique and original?
6. What were some of the messages and backgrounds of Israel's prophets?
7. What was the ultimate goal of the prophets?
8. When you hear the word *prophet* what words or images come to mind?
9. What lessons can we learn from the life of Elijah?
10. Tell what impresses you most about Elijah.

Prayer

Dear God, thank you for giving us voices that remind us of you and tell us of your love and goodness. Amen.

CHAPTER 9
PETER, JAMES, AND JOHN: BRINGING IN THE KINGDOM

Snapshot Summary

This chapter looks at the twelve men selected by Jesus to be his disciples, with a special focus on Peter, James, and John.

Reflection / Discussion Questions

1. Why is the number twelve so significant, and how is it repeated in the Bible?
2. Give an overview of the apostles' qualifications and background.
3. Consider and explain the connection and importance of leader and follower.

4. Name some of the reasons Jesus chose these twelve men.

5. How were the apostles similar to and different from one another?

6. Explain how these men were prepared for ministry. What gifts did they possess?

7. Why is it important that all twelve men were seekers?

8. What impresses you most about these men and their accomplishments?

9. Why were they successful in their mission?

10. Explain why the author names this chapter after three apostles: Peter, James, and John. List some of their contributions.

Prayer

Dear God, thank you for calling us to share your word with others, giving us the example of your twelve disciples. Amen.

CHAPTER 10
MARTHA, AND SEVERAL MARYS: THEY ALSO SERVE WHO ONLY STAND AND SERVE

Snapshot Summary

This chapter looks at the key women of the Bible. It includes their contributions, service to others, faith, and encounters with Jesus.

Reflection / Discussion Questions

1. Name some key women who have made our world a better place.

2. List some of the women in the Bible who made important contributions.

3. Why was it daring for the apostle Paul to announce a new era in Galatians 3:28?
4. What roles did Mary and Elizabeth play in the biblical plot and story?
5. Why are the words "many women" significant in Matthew's account of the Crucifixion?
6. In your own words, explain what it means to serve.
7. Explain the role women played in the Easter story.
8. What "first" did Anna perform after seeing the baby Jesus?
9. Jesus encountered and interacted with many women in his ministry. Describe some of these encounters.
10. What lessons about service and serving others can we learn from these women?

Prayer

Dear God, thank you for the many contributions and the faith of women who teach us how to be better Christians.

CHAPTER 11
PAUL: THE PERIPATETIC THEOLOGIAN

Snapshot Summary

This chapter is about the life and ministry of the apostle Paul and how he was used by God to further God's kingdom.

Reflection / Discussion Questions

1. Explain why you can't ignore Paul in telling the biblical story.

2. What is known about Paul as a person? List his several names and explain them.
3. In what ways was Saul involved in the stoning of Stephen?
4. What impresses you about the conversion of Saul?
5. Describe what obstacles Paul faced after his conversion.
6. Why do some people call Paul the first Christian missionary?
7. How was Paul different from the other disciples?
8. List some of Paul's accomplishments.
9. What do you admire most about Paul?
10. Name some lessons we can learn from Paul's life and his ministry.

Prayer

Dear God, thank you for the life, witness, and example of Paul, your faithful servant. Help us continue his work. Amen.

CHAPTER 12
JESUS CHRIST: THE SON OF GOD AND THE SON OF HUMANITY

Snapshot Summary

This final chapter explores the life and impact of Jesus, our Lord, Savior, and friend.

Reflection / Discussion Questions

1. What thoughts come to mind after reading "One Solitary Life"?
2. Why was the life of Jesus both memorable and commonplace?
3. Who followed Jesus and why?

4. Why and how did Jesus become a polarizing figure?
5. Who felt threatened by Jesus and why?
6. Why do you think Jesus performed miracles?
7. How is it that Jesus Christ continues to gain such a following today? Why is there such a hunger for him?
8. Who is Jesus? List some of the many answers and identities.
9. Why do you believe in Jesus?
10. What new insights did you receive from reading this book?

Prayer

Dear God, thank you for giving us Jesus to love, protect, sustain, and forgive us. Amen.